In these shoes?!

Shell Perris

First published 2005
ISBN 1 84427 140 4

Scripture Union, 207–209 Queensway, Bletchley,
Milton Keynes, MK2 2EB, England.
Email: info@scriptureunion.org.uk
Website: www.scriptureunion.org.uk

Scripture Union Australia
Locked Bag 2, Central Coast Business Centre, NSW 2252
Website: www.scriptureunion.org.au

Scripture Union USA
PO Box 987, Valley Forge, PA 19482
Website: www.scriptureunion.org

British Library Cataloguing-in-Publication Data.
A catalogue record of this book is available from the British Library.

Printed and bound in Great Britain by
Creative Print and Design (Wales) Ebbw Vale.

Cover and internal design: Martin Lore

Scripture Union is an international Christian charity working with churches in more than 130 countries, providing resources to bring the good news about Jesus Christ to children, young people and families and to encourage them to develop spiritually through the Bible and prayer.

As well as our network of volunteers, staff and associates who run holidays, church-based events and school Christian groups, we produce a wide range of publications and support those who use our resources through training programmes.

Contents

Introduction

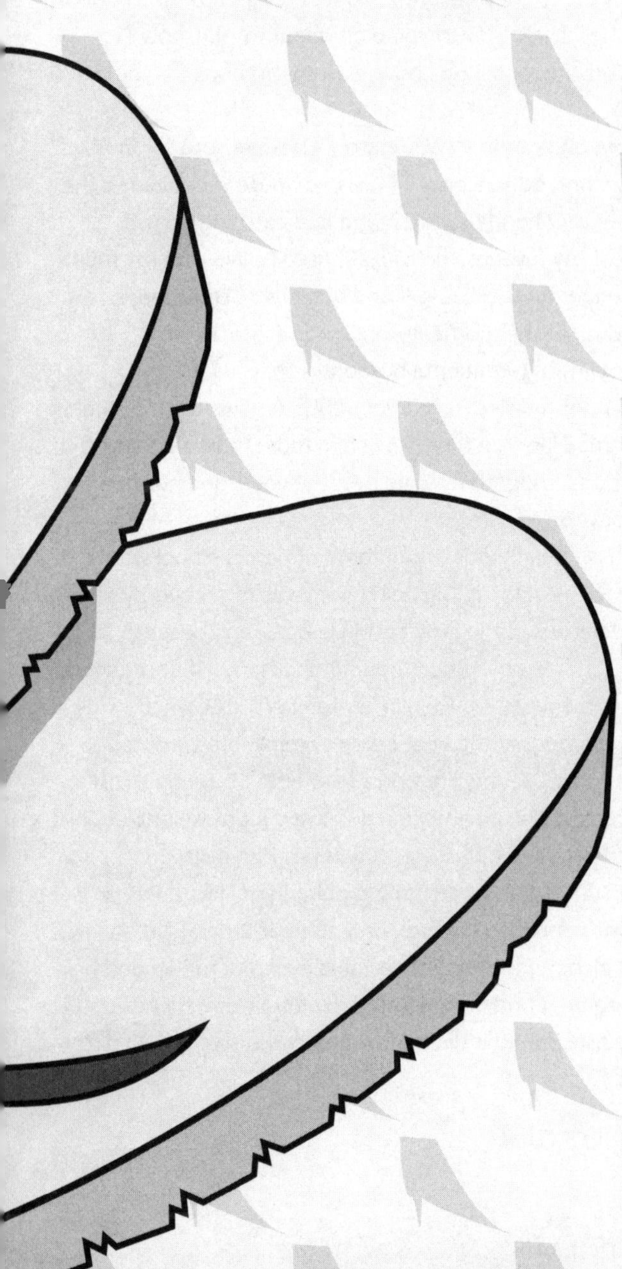

Introduction

As you've probably guessed by the name on the front of this book, I'm called Shell. I want to tell you a bit about my life, how I became a Christian and why I have written this book for you. So here goes!

I was born and raised in Warrington, Cheshire, and for most of my childhood and adolescence I lived in a house very close to the town centre – very handy for shopping and catching up with friends, two of my favourite activities! I used to live with my mum, dad and younger brother Craig – and of course I can't forget Shanti, the dog. At the moment I am living in Stockport, Manchester, with my wonderful husband Tim.

Tim and I got married in February 2005 and we are thoroughly enjoying married life together. I love him more than anything. Tim has been a huge inspiration to me over the years and has had a massive impact on my life.

Although my childhood was fantastic at home, school was always hard for me. During the first three years of secondary school I was bullied because I tried my best in lessons, and because I was thin. It really affected the way I thought about myself. It made me feel useless and unwanted. Then in September 1999, when I was 15, I stopped eating. At the time I didn't realise, but I wanted to have some control over my life, and I felt I didn't have any. For three months I hardly ate anything and lost a lot of weight, until I only weighed six and a half stone. It was a cry for help.

January 2000 was a huge turning point in my life. I was diagnosed with anorexia nervosa, an eating disorder. I felt so low that I'd lost all hope that anything could ever pick me up and help me to start again. I had disappointed my family and friends and I had been selfish. But little did I know that being so ill would direct me to Jesus.

I met a few guys, Steve, Jon and Tim (who is now my husband). They were all Christians and had a lot to do with an organisation called YFC. I'd seen Steve around my school before because he was a youth worker there, but I'd never felt the urge to go and speak to him. But on one particular day, I knew I had to. I told him exactly how I was feeling and what was going on in my life. That's when I became a Christian.

To cut a very long story short, a lot of things have happened since then and my relationship with God has grown so much. God has led me through good times and bad times, and he has shaped me into the person I am today. When I was first led to Jesus, Steve said this:

'Here I am! I stand at the door and knock. If you hear my voice and open the door, I will come in and eat with you, and you will eat with me.'

(Revelation 3:20)

Little did I know that this verse would have such an impact on every aspect of my life!

At the moment, I am working for an organisation called Innervation Trust, an organisation that is dedicated to presenting the Gospel of Jesus Christ to thousands of young people in schools throughout the UK. I am part of "tbc" – one of the Innervation touring bands. (Look at page 111 for more info on Innervation Trust's work.) I am so privileged to have the opportunity to tell young people about Jesus and give them hope for the future.

As I have visited schools over the last few years, God has enabled me to use my experiences to help other people and that is partly why I have written this book. I hope that as you read it, my personal stories and God's Word will challenge you, minister to you, comfort you and inspire you.

When I was struggling with my eating disorder, I needed to feel that I had the support of someone who really understood what I was going through – someone who knew what it was like to be in my shoes, and could help me on my journey. I hope that 'In these shoes?' will encourage and support you on your journey through adolescence.

'Praise be to the God and Father of our Lord Jesus Christ. God is the Father who is full of mercy and all comfort. He comforts us every time we have trouble, so when others have trouble, we can comfort them with the same comfort God gives us.'

(2 Corinthians 1:3,4)

11

In these shoes?!

Chapter 1:
Shoes for show: Self-image

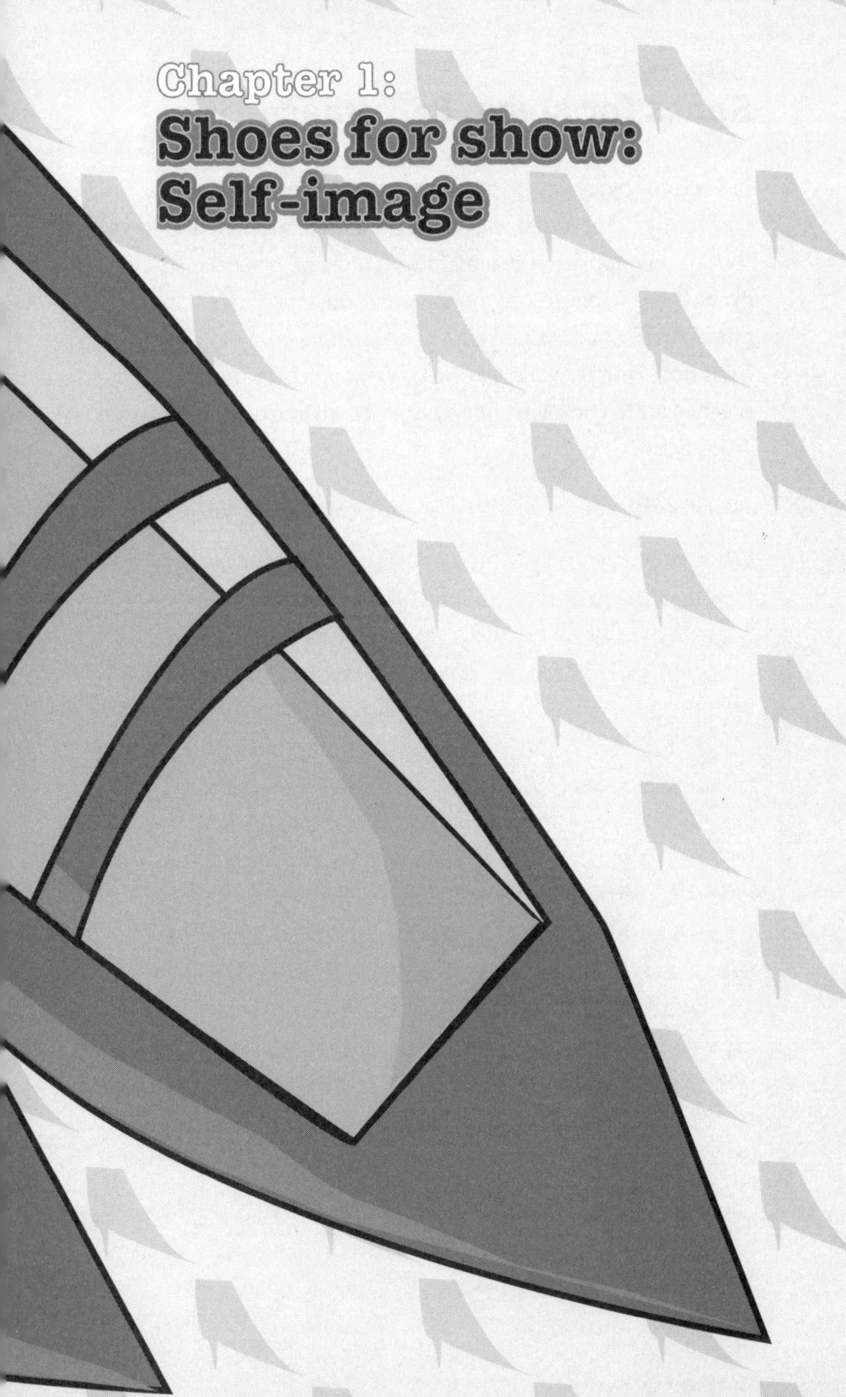

Chapter 1:
Shoes for show: Self-image

It's sad to think that we live in a society where people are constantly bombarded with a message that supports the idea that to be happy and successful you must be a certain size. It's everywhere – magazines, newspapers, advertisements and television. From as young as 3 years, people are being told that fat is bad. From a worldly point of view, if you're thin and pretty, you're complete, happy and secure in everything you do. True? False.

!

We are constantly bombarded with messages from the media. Advertising alone is a multi-million pound business, and its sole aim is to entice the general public into buying particular products by whatever means necessary. Advertisers achieve their object by splattering our screens with images of the ideal body. It doesn't matter what the product is – everything from chocolate bars to cars to washing machines includes perfect curves, complexions and cheekbones. The underlying message is, 'If you buy this perfume, you too will have the allure of Kate Moss' or 'If you drive this car, women will fall at your feet'.

Unfortunately, advertising has a dangerous side effect. Normal people like us, compare our bodies to the models we see in those adverts, the movies and the magazines and we think, 'I don't look like that!' The media screams at our subconscious,

'You're not good enough, you're ugly. You need to look like this.'

Steve Mawston, 'Who Do You Think You Are?'
Scripture Union, 1997 (out of print)

The truth is that you don't need to compare yourself to anyone. Most of the images you see in magazines and on the television are computer enhanced anyway. Just be who you are! God wouldn't want it any other way.

You don't need to compare yourself to anyone. Just be who you are!

The dress code

'Also, women should wear proper clothes that show respect and self-control, not using plaited hair or gold or pearls or expensive clothes. Instead, they should do good deeds, which is right for women who say they worship God.'

(1 Timothy 2:9,10)

I remember reaching a stage in my life where I wanted to look as good as I possibly could. I was about 13 when I realised that if I wore a short skirt or a skimpy top, boys would look at me and find me attractive. I wanted attention from the lads, and I enjoyed getting it because it was a massive confidence boost. What I didn't realise at the time was that it was a distraction to the lads, and very negative for me.

Let's explore the things that can happen when a girl wears a short skirt and a revealing top.

1) Although you might feel amazing, boys will undoubtedly look at you and think you're up for it. This could lead to many situations that you wouldn't want to find yourself in, but can be very difficult to get out of.

2) It says in the Bible, 'But I tell you that if anyone looks at a woman and wants to sin sexually with her, in his mind he has already done that sin with the woman.' (Matthew 5:28). So by dressing inappropriately, girls may be tempting lads to go against God's Word. That may sound a little harsh but some men are lacking in the self-control department and we shouldn't do anything to make that worse for them.

3) If you make a habit of wearing skimpy clothes, you could gain a reputation that would make things difficult later on in life. For example, if you turn up showing loads of flesh, people could associate you with some nasty words. You can probably guess what they might be.

God thinks you're beautiful no matter what!

This isn't to say that you can't look nice! Everyone wants to look nice and feel good, but there is a fine line. I have learned a lot since being in a band. If we were to wear low-cut tops or figure-hugging trousers on stage, the boys would have something to look at, and it would be a huge distraction to the message we are trying to give out. It would almost be hypocritical. We would be telling people about Jesus and how you shouldn't lust, but at the same time, tempting lads to lust because of the way we dressed. It doesn't fit! It's important to know that you can look just as good by wearing clothes that cover you up and don't show too much flesh. When I'm trying clothes on in a shop I tend to think to myself, if Jesus was right here right now, would I wear this outfit in front of him? If the answer is yes, then if I like it I buy it. If the answer is no, then it goes straight back on the hanger. Remember that God thinks you're beautiful no matter what, and that's all that matters!

Prayer

Lord,

Thank you that I don't have to compare myself to anyone because in your eyes I am beautiful no matter what! Thank you that I am special to you.

Help me to dress in a way that glorifies you and makes me feel good.

In Jesus' name,

Amen.

My story

During my secondary school years I was constantly bullied because I was thin. People would call me names like Twiggy and Stick. It hurt me so much. Being thin would be some people's idea of paradise but it certainly wasn't mine. I wanted a bigger chest, straighter hair, curvier hips, a smaller nose…

I didn't have many friends at school. I was one of those girls who always handed homework in on time, was quiet and hard working in lessons and did extra-curricular activities at least twice a week. People seemed to think that because I was thin and achieved good grades, I was secure and happy with myself. In fact, I was quite the opposite. I felt lonely, insecure, worthless and unloved. I felt sick every morning at the thought of having to go to school and face the people in my class.

When I was 15, I woke up one morning and looked at myself in the mirror with such disappointment and unhappiness. I wanted things to be different. I longed to go to school and fit in with everyone else. I was crying out for a sense of belonging. I felt that I had no control over my life and the things that I did. So I stopped eating. Eating was the one thing that only I could control; no one could make me eat if I didn't want to.

Every morning, my mum would make my lunch. I'd put it in my bag and then as soon as I got to school I would throw it in the bin. At least that way, even if I was hungry at lunch, I wouldn't be able to eat anything because I wouldn't have anything. In the morning I would go downstairs half an hour before anyone else, and make it look as if I'd had some breakfast. At night I would complain that I wasn't feeling well or I didn't like what we were having, or say I'd had tea at one of my friend's houses.

For three months, I got worse and worse and survived most of the day on chewing gum and drinks. My periods had virtually stopped and only lasted a day, if that. My skin was covered with patches of skin pigments because I hadn't been having any vitamins. I was continually exhausted and never had any energy. I was at the bottom of the pit, and I didn't know how to get out of it. Eventually, my mum and dad found out. They tried to force-feed me and they threatened to take me to the doctors, but I still wouldn't eat. I felt an overwhelming sense of power. I had defeated my parents and gained control over my actions, or so I thought. But my parents dragged me to the doctors. The doctor weighed me and found that I was well below the weight I should have been. He looked me in the eye and told me I had anorexia nervosa. He said that I'd knocked years off my expected lifespan because I had put so much pressure on my heart. He said that when I eventually want to have children it will be harder to get pregnant. I sat there in shock. I looked over to my mum and dad and saw the shock and disappointment on their faces.

The doctors referred me to a counsellor at the local hospital. After going there for a while, I realised that I needed something more than the help of my counsellor, friends and family. There was something still missing. At that point, I was reminded of all the Bible verses Steve, Jon and Tim had given me, and I realised that Jesus was the only person who was going to bring me through my eating disorder. So I said a prayer and I asked Jesus to be my best mate and help me. I knew at that moment that if I were to struggle with my eating again, Jesus was always going to be there to pick me up and help me. Even better than that, if I was ever to struggle with anything, Jesus was always going to be there.

I believe that Jesus has healed me from anorexia. If I'm honest, I still have the odd day when I struggle to eat, but in those situations I just turn to Jesus and remember how he brought me through anorexia and how he can also bring me through a bad day.

When I became a Christian, the bullying at school didn't happen as much. People respected me more. I had lots of friends and I actually enjoyed going to school. Jesus helped me to be more confident in myself, which made such a massive impact on my life and on other people's lives.

In the Bible, there are many stories of how Jesus healed people. For example, he made a blind man see again; he gave a deaf man the ability to hear again; and he helped a man to walk. There's a story of a woman who had been bleeding for 12 years and just by touching Jesus' coat she was healed. Jesus even brought people back to life. He can do anything!

'... The LORD says this to you: "Don't be afraid or discouraged because of this large army. The battle is not your battle, it is God's."'
(2 Chronicles 20:15)

Anorexia was a challenging illness to get through. I had my good days and my bad days. I saw paediatricians, dietitians, family psychologists and counsellors.

I made that one decision to control how much food I ate and then spent the next two years of my life trying to undo the consequences of my actions.

'When a person's steps follow the LORD,
God is pleased with his ways.
If he stumbles, he will not fall,
because the LORD holds his hand.'
(Psalm 37:23,24)

How amazing is that! To think that in every situation, whether it's good or bad, Jesus is prepared to hold our hand. He is prepared to walk through it with us from beginning to end. It's so comforting to know that God sent his one and only son, Jesus, to die on the cross in such a painful way, so that in every single situation we have ever faced or will ever face, he can guide us through.

'... God called you to be free ...'
(Galatians 5:13)

If I were to sit here and say that anorexia isn't an issue for me any more, I'd be lying. Sometimes I still find it difficult to eat a certain thing, but it's during those times that I turn to the Bible and recognise the freedom that God has given me.

'I can do all things through Christ, because he gives me strength.'
(Philippians 4:13)

I have so many stories of how God has taken my experience of having anorexia, and used it to help other people by allowing me to tell them about what Jesus has done in my life. Some people seem amazed that Christians go through hard times and have problems just like everyone else. The difference is that Christians have something to hold on to – an everlasting love and a peace that outshines everything. What more could you ask for?

Made in God's image

'It is not fancy hair, gold jewellery or fine clothes that should make you beautiful. No, your beauty should come from within you — the beauty of a gentle and quiet spirit that will never be destroyed and is very precious to God.'
(1 Peter 3:3,4)

When we girls get upset and start shouting, 'Why does no one understand me?' we can be sure that there's one person who does – God!

Isn't it fantastic to know that God loves us just the way we are, more than we can possibly imagine? We don't have to hide our blemishes or have a shower for God to love us. When I wake up in the morning, I can almost guarantee that the first five minutes will be used to define what I have to do in order to make myself feel and look a little less scruffy!

God knows exactly how many hairs we have on our head, and in the emotional times when we get upset and start shouting, 'Why does no one understand me?' we can be assured that there's one person who does – God!

'So God created human beings in his image. In the image of God he created them. He created them male and female.'
(Genesis 1:27)

We have all been created in God's image. There is something of God in our human characteristics and we each have a unique individuality. It's hard to believe that every single human being in the whole entire world has a different thumbprint. We have all been designed for different reasons, and that's the amazing bit.

'God has made us what we are. In Christ Jesus, God made us to do good works ... '
(Ephesians 2:10)

'God has made us what we are ... '
(Ephesians 2:10)

The thing that never fails to amaze me is that no matter how many times we mess up, 'In Christ Jesus, God made us ... ' That means that when we become a Christian, God sees us as a new person. And he loves us just as we are, no matter what we look like to the outside world. Through his son dying on the cross, even though we don't deserve it, we can receive forgiveness and acceptance that only God can give.

Prayer

Lord,

Thank you that you are prepared to love me just the way I am. Thank you that I am your masterpiece! Thank you that you died on the cross for me so that I could be forgiven for all the things I have ever done wrong and will ever do wrong.

Help me to be a girl of God in every area of my life.

In Jesus' name,

Amen.

Want to know more...?

Taming the Lion *Cathie Bartlam*

A dramatic story of one girl's battle with bulimia (fiction).

Scripture Union 1 85999 054 1

Hidden Hunger *Maxine Davies*

Intended for adults but easy to read. Offers profound insight into breaking free from eating disorders with God's help.

Authentic Lifestyle 1 86024 296 0

81 per cent of 10-year-old girls are afraid of being fat
(Mellin et al, 1991)
Most fashion models are thinner than
98 per cent of American women
(Smolak, 1996)
51 per cent of 9- and 10-year-old girls feel better about themselves if they are on a diet
(Mellin et al, 1991)

!

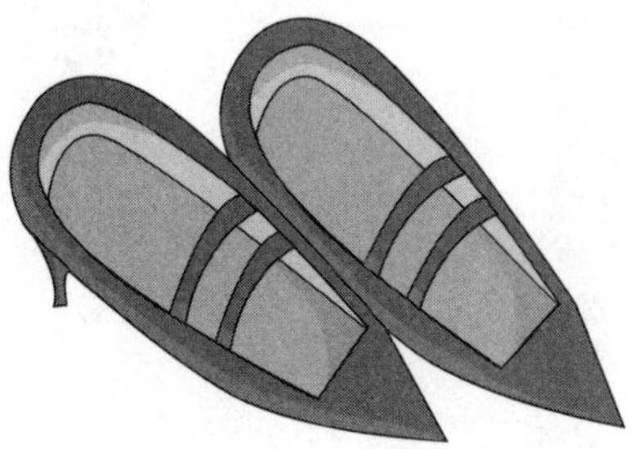

In these shoes?!

Chapter 2:
Winkle-pickers and stilettos: Dealing with painful pressures

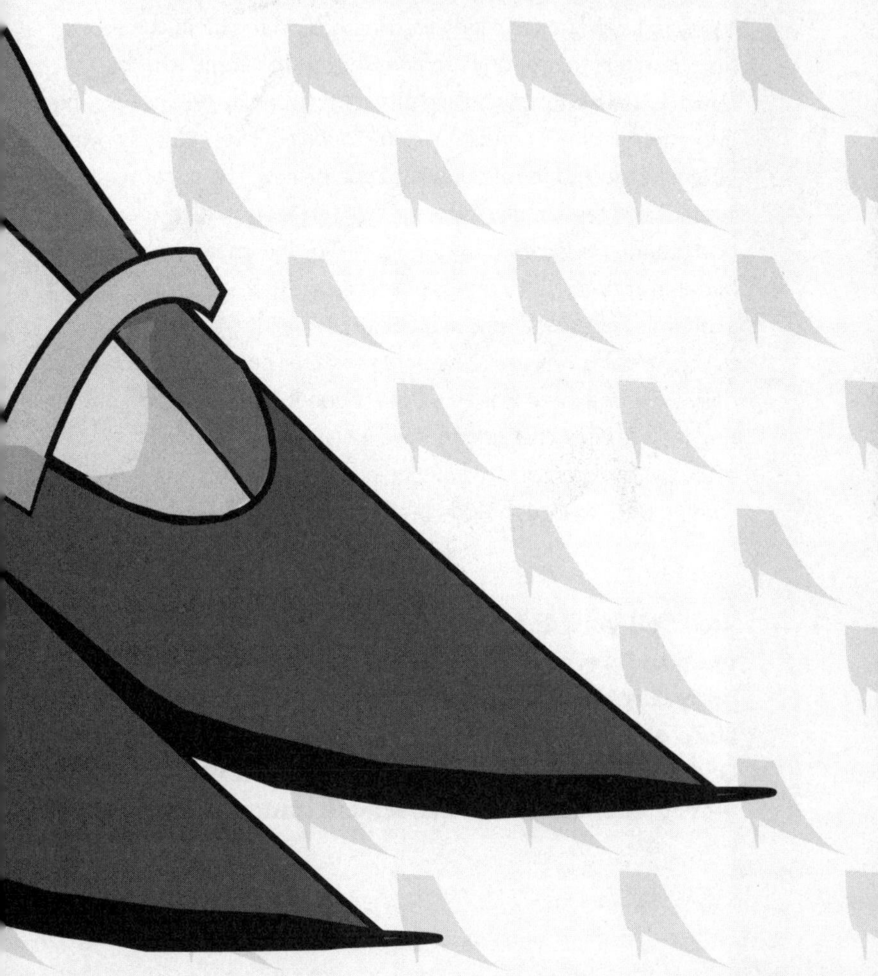

Chapter 2:
Winkle-pickers and stilettos: Dealing with painful pressures

Stress!

AAhhh! Do you ever feel that life is just too much? That no matter how hard you try, things are just that little bit out of reach? I know I have times when the pressures of life seem to take over: I'm trying to keep one too many juggling balls in the air at the same time, and feel that at any moment they will all come crashing down. It's not only general life pressures (work/life balance etc) but also other people's unrealistic expectations of me – plus my own internal expectations about what I can achieve – that cause me stress. As a teenage girl, I was easily influenced by all the background pressures in my life. As well as the image issue I talked about in chapter 1, there was peer pressure, parental pressure, academic pressure, financial pressure… The list goes on.

The Bible is very realistic about pressures people face in their daily lives, and Jesus was very honest about their existence, plus the need to keep checking that we have our priorities right. He often took himself off to a quiet place to think and pray, before coming back to face the clamouring crowds again.

'So I tell you, don't worry about the food or drink you need to live, or about the clothes you need for your body. Life is more than food, and the body is more than clothes ... The thing you should want most is God's kingdom and doing what God wants ... So don't worry about tomorrow, because tomorrow will have

its own worries. Each day has enough trouble of its own.'

(Matthew 6:25-34)

When I read those Bible verses, they put everything into perspective. Some things just aren't worth worrying about. I'm too good at worrying about things that I don't need to worry about. God clearly says in that passage that first of all we should want his kingdom and doing what he wants of us. I know I definitely need to focus more on that. Maybe then I wouldn't spend as much time worrying about the things I can't change.

'Early the next morning, while it was still dark, Jesus woke and left the house. He went to a lonely place, where he prayed.'

(Mark 1:35)

Jesus was such an inspirational man. His whole life reflected the work of God in so many ways. He spent the majority of his time just praying and seeking God. There are so many times when I find myself using the excuse of not having enough time to do a Bible study, or not having enough time to pray and seek God, but Jesus made time. God was at the top of his priority list and nothing ever replaced him. Maybe it would be a good idea to sit down and think about what is at the top of your priority list. Is Jesus number one?

People's expectations of women in the church

This is one of those subjects where there are a lot of different attitudes and opinions. Believe me, it can be stressful trying to live up to other people's expectations! It is a good idea to think about the different issues yourself, look up relevant Bible passages and have honest discussions with people you trust and respect. For example, some people think that women should be free to take any leadership position within the church, and some people think that it's a man's role. There are actually aspects of both in the Bible.

'In Christ, there is no difference between Jew and Greek, slave and free person, male and female. You are all the same in Christ Jesus.'
(Galatians 3:28)

In this passage, it states that both men and women are equal. I have led worship, preached and counselled people of all ages and I have felt that God has been there with me all the way. So, personally, I think that women, along with men, can have huge potential when it comes to leadership. But I know that other Christians disapprove of women in church leadership. You'll need to decide for yourself by talking to God about it and reading the Bible.

Our society has changed so much in the last 60 years! Whereas our grandmothers may have expected to be housewives and child bearers, today's women may decide to go to university and have careers, then perhaps get married and have children a lot later on. Women are taking on much more responsibility outside the home and it's bound to affect the church.

'After this, while Jesus was travelling through some cities and small towns, he preached and told the Good News about God's kingdom. The twelve apostles were with him, and also some women who had been healed of sicknesses and evil spirits: Mary, called Magdalene, from whom seven demons had gone out; Joanna, the wife of Chuza (the manager of Herod's house); Susanna; and many others. These women used their own money to help Jesus and his apostles.'

(Luke 8:1-3)

As you probably know yourself, girls can be very sensitive, both emotionally and spiritually, and this can be a very positive quality. It says in the passage above that women accompanied Jesus so that they could support him and his disciples. Back in those days, women obviously played a very important role in the ministry of Jesus, but he was always the boss. It's sometimes the same today; men can be seen as the 'head' in a church, but that doesn't necessarily mean that women have no authority there.

Walk away

I would like to share with you the words of a song I wrote about a girl who found herself fighting against pressures of teenage life:

Everlasting memories,
A cry of loneliness.
Her heart is filled with so much pain,
Her mind's already dead.
She's living in a nightmare,
'Cause she couldn't say that word.
If only she'd heard.

So much of life's been wasted,
She's barely 17.
The whole world there beneath her feet.
She was diving in too deep.
She knew there was a problem,
But she'd say it was okay. She'd say,
'I want you, so please don't walk away.'

You said that you'd never be
Afraid to believe
You can do all things.
I knew you right from the start.
I knew your heart,
But where are you now?'

Actions that have stolen
The joy within her soul.

The life she lives is cold.
They tried to tell her not to,
But every day she'd say,
'I need you, so please don't walk away.'

Everlasting memories.
A cry of loneliness.
Her heart was filled with so much pain.
Her mind was already dead.
She was living in a nightmare.
If only she could say, 'No,
I'm sorry, I have to walk away.'

The girl in this song began, like me, by wanting something. Then the 'you' (the problem, whether it be an eating disorder, sex, self-harm, excessive drinking, attention-seeking, low self-esteem, etc) took over her life and killed her, leaving it too late to walk away. A girl who set out longing for freedom ended up being a slave to the problem.

Are there things or areas in your life that have started off as little things that you want but, without you realising it, have turned into things that you need and can't seem to live without? Are they making you feel stressed and holding you back from the many plans and purposes that God has for your life? Well, this is the time to deal with them and learn to live in freedom. Don't feel ashamed of yourself because you have a problem. One of the reasons I didn't want to admit that I had anorexia was because I felt ashamed and I was frightened of what people would think of me. When I finally did admit it, I was surprised by their reactions. They were really supportive and understanding. People didn't judge me because of my situation. They just loved me through it.

What can you do?

Well, the first thing you need to do is find out whether or not you have a problem. Don't go looking for things and think that it's wrong not to have a problem. It's fine! But if you are struggling with something, here are a few bits of advice to help you deal with the pressure along the way:

- Pray – The most important thing to do is to make God aware of exactly how you are feeling. Tell him everything. Ask him to help you and comfort you.
- Find someone to talk to – Find someone you can trust and who is a few years older than you, and talk to them about how you're feeling. They will be able to pray with you and maybe even suggest ways of helping you through it. Remember what I said before: don't feel ashamed! The chances are that there are other people going through exactly the same things you are.
- Read about other people's experiences – It's important to understand that you are not alone. Not only is God with you, but other people will be able to use their own experiences to help you too. Go to your nearest Christian bookshop and find a book that will help you (there is a list of great, encouraging books at the end of this chapter to help get you started).

Prayer

Lord,

Thank you that whatever is happening in my life, I don't have to deal with it on my own. Thank you that I don't have to feel ashamed because I know that you will always love me, no matter what.

Help me to be honest with you and with myself.

In the name of Jesus,

Amen.

Want to know more...?

Under Pressure *Claire Pedrick + Andy Morgan*

The ultimate pressure survival guide!

Exams, parents, the future, life…!

Scripture Union 1 84427 008 4

One-up

Essential regular help with Bible reading and prayer.

Scripture Union 1360 3051

Airlock: *Arrival*

Bible reading for older teens.

Scripture Union 184427 047 5

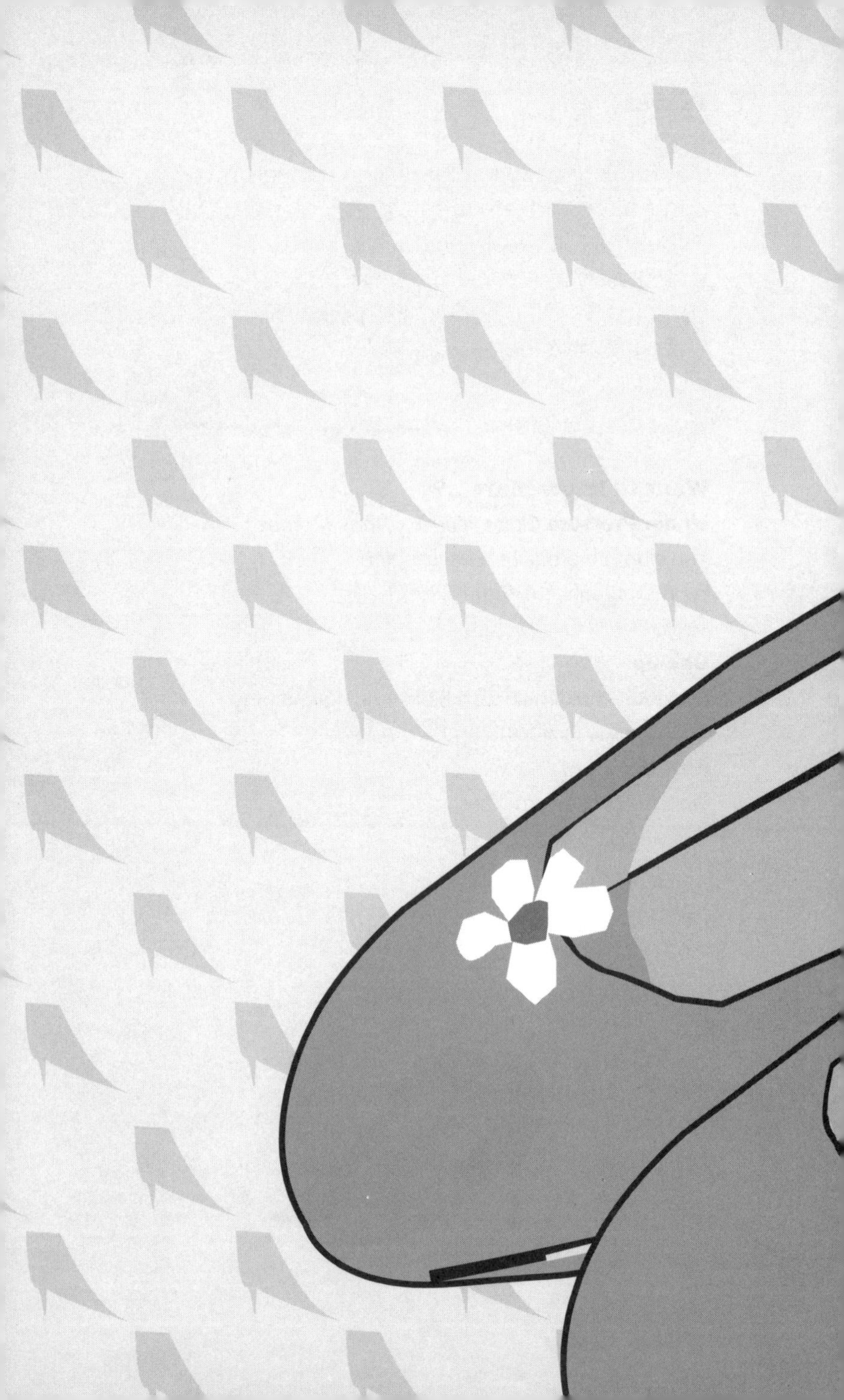

Chapter 3:
'Where are my slippers?' Dealing with insecurities

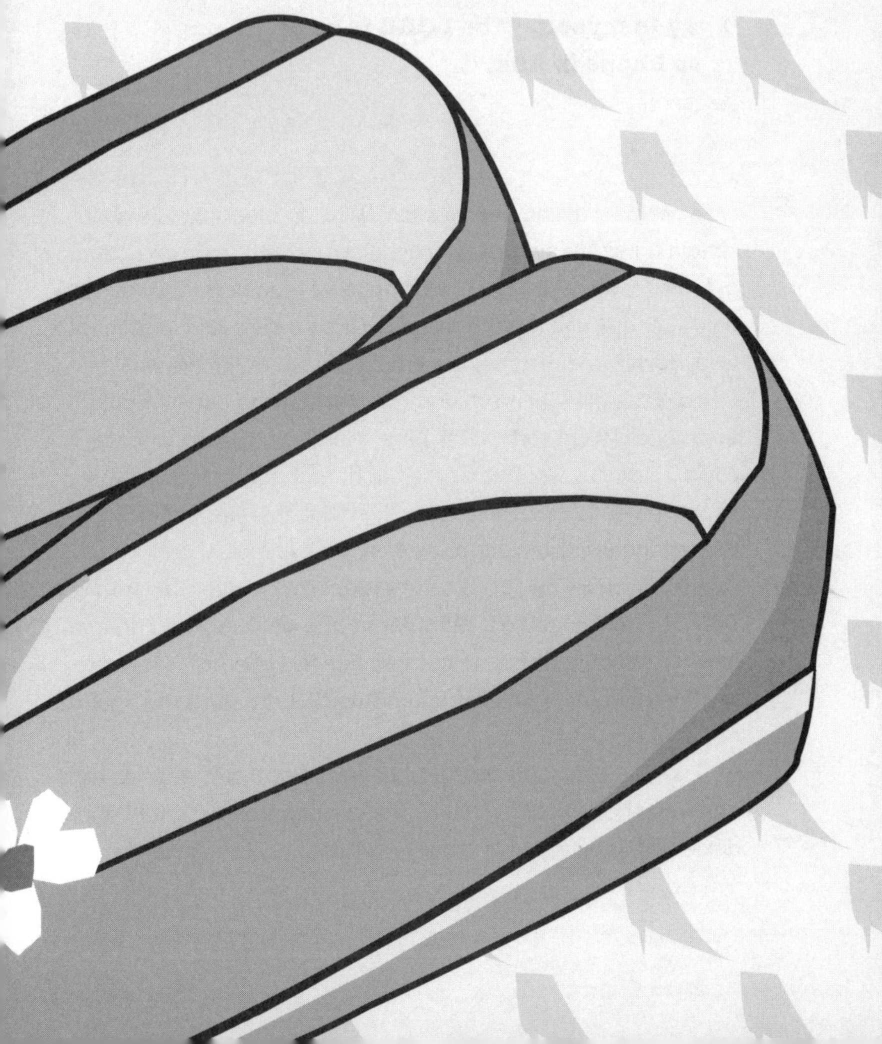

Chapter 3:
'Where are my slippers?' Dealing with insecurities

Insecurity

I want to remind you of some very powerful words from the Bible:

'I say to myself, "The LORD is mine,
so I hope in him."'
(Lamentations 3:24)

Let's begin by asking the question: 'Why do I feel insecure about certain things in my life?' As a general rule, with some exceptions, girls are far more sensitive and emotional than boys. This can often be a strength, and may enable us to have a deep relationship with God. However, sometimes our emotions can totally overwhelm us.

For example, when Tim and I were first going out, he would occasionally want some 'Tim Time' – time on his own, when he could do exactly what he wanted to do without having to think about someone else. Looking back on that, it seems perfectly understandable. However, there were many times when I would take it personally and become insecure in my relationship with him. I used to think to myself, 'Why doesn't he want to spend time with me?' or 'What have I done to make him feel like this?' I failed to see it from his point of view and instead, let my insecurities get the better of me.

Insecurities can distract us from what God wants us to do with our lives. They can quickly turn into jealousy, loneliness, hurt and anxiety. It's so easy to find our security in people instead of in God and it's sometimes easier to tell other people about our problems before we tell God. This isn't to say that God doesn't want us to confide in other people – the Bible encourages us to surround ourselves with friends and share in the community. However, it is important to realise that God loves us more than anyone else possibly could and he alone can give us what we need. It is only in God that we can find complete security.

God is our rock in times of trouble.

'Don't be too proud in the Lord's presence, and he will make you great.'
(James 4:10)

But how do I get complete security in God?

To get complete security in God we have to open our heart to him and allow him to make the difference in our lives. To reach our potential, we have to let his love shine and continually warm us through. We have to want to get rid of the insecurities and allow him to change us in dramatic and small ways. We have to allow him to deal with each aspect of our life, even if that means being broken and then being reformed.

Once Jesus is at the centre of your life, no limits can be put on the works of God through you.

My minister once told me that our lives are like houses. Every part of our life is a different room, and our heart is the front door. Every room has a door and a key, and Jesus wants to hold the key to each one, not just the front door. Jesus wants to hold the keys to our friendships, our schoolwork, our family, our thoughts, our desires and our dreams.

We have to allow Jesus into every room, even if that means visiting past events that have been brushed under the carpet, or entering rooms you didn't even know existed. But it is only then that we can begin to fulfil the purposes God has for us and enter into a refreshing security with God. Once Jesus is truly at the centre of our life, no limits can be put on the works of God through us.

Steps to security in God

- God accepts us as we are, but over time God changes things in our life in order to complete his promises – we are a new creation in him. We need to allow God to make adjustments to our way of thinking.
- We must learn to let go of the things that are holding us back from achieving that complete security that he has freely offered to us. This may be one of the hardest things we ever have to do, as we follow him and trust that what he has in store is worth fighting for.
- We need to learn to leave the past behind and concentrate on the future. God allows us to go through difficult times for so many reasons, including preparation for the future, teaching us to rely on God and not on ourselves, getting to know who we are and what we stand for, bringing to light all that's hidden in our lives so that we can move on and change, helping us to know and appreciate God's Word and helping us to gain maturity and experience.

- We must learn to sense the quiet whisper of God as he guides us, and always want to be in his presence.
- Keep going! It is only by having a real friendship with Jesus that we are able to achieve and take hold of that complete security that God gives us.

!

Take some time out to reflect on areas of your life where you are feeling insecure and need God's grace.

Prayer

Lord Jesus,

Thank you that in you I can feel secure and complete. Thank you that you love me for who I am. Help me to allow you into every area of my life, especially the areas I haven't let you into before.

(You might want to tell Jesus about certain areas of your life as they come to mind, eg 'My relationship with my parents', 'Schoolwork'. Remember, this is personal to you, so tell him about the things that apply to you – you don't have to use these examples.)

I want your love to shine through every single bit of my life.

In your name,

Amen.

Setting the trend

When I was at secondary school, knee-length skirts were a part of the school uniform. However, at the time, miniskirts were in fashion. All the other girls wore really short skirts, but my mum was always telling me how important it was that I followed the rules and wore a knee-length skirt. I hated it. So I would walk downstairs for breakfast with a knee-length skirt on. As soon as I was out of sight, I would stop and roll my skirt up a few inches. No one ever mentioned my skirt at school because it was like everyone else's. I would walk around feeling more confident in the fact that I was wearing a short skirt, like everyone else.

Looking back on it, I realise that I just wanted to follow the crowd. I wanted to feel as if I belonged. I was a sheep!

!

If you walk around doing what everyone else does and saying what everyone else says, you will never find out who you are and what your real purpose is in life.

Individuality is what makes a person. If you walk around doing what everyone else does and saying what everyone else says, you will never find out who you are and what your real purpose is in life. It's healthy to look up to people and be inspired by them, but it is sometimes unhealthy to follow them and their ways. It might not be what God has planned for you! As you grow up, there will be times in your life when you feel that you have to go along with something you're not entirely sure about. You might be following the crowd if you are:

- Being mean to someone who isn't very popular.
- Wearing clothing/accessories that are banned at school.
- Staying out later than your parents want you to.

What do you think?

Know that God has made you the way you are. Don't ever be ashamed of that!

Who are you?

1) Do you know who you are?

Who are you? What excites you? What makes you happy or unhappy? What is it you're living for? What are your characteristics? What is it about you that makes you who you are?

For years I thought I knew who I was and what I wanted, until someone challenged me on it. It turned out that deep down inside I was very unsure. It wasn't until I found my security in God that I knew the answers to some of those questions. I learned that God can do so much more when we step outside our comfort zones.

2) Do you know what you want?

What do you want from your life? Where do you want to be in ten years' time? What are your dreams and ambitions? How are you going to achieve them? Try asking God for guidance, and make him aware that you are ready and willing to use your dreams and talents to glorify him.

God can do so much more when we step outside our comfort zones.

If you know who you are and what you want, that's fantastic! Keep going! But if you don't know the answers to those two questions, I would suggest that you sit down with someone you respect and trust, and ask them to help you. God will carry you through times of uncertainty and confusion.

'The LORD hears good people when they cry out to him,
and he saves them from all their troubles.
The LORD is close to the broken-hearted,
and he saves those whose spirits have been crushed.'
(Psalm 34:17,18)

How do you hear God's voice?

This is a question I get asked time and time again by kids in schools.

There are many different ways to hear God. Some people do experience audible words. However, sometimes it might be a gut feeling, when you just know that it's God saying something to you. Sometimes God might speak to you through a Bible verse. You could be reading the Bible and all of a sudden one specific verse seems to jump out at you; you read it and it's exactly what you needed to hear. Sometimes God might speak to you through a dream, a picture or a vision. Sometimes God might speak to you through someone else; he might give them a Bible verse to give to you. God can speak to you in many different ways. The most important thing is to learn when it's God saying something to you, and when it's actually you just thinking something. That comes with practice. There will be times when you get it wrong, but don't worry. It's a learning process.

You are so talented!

'Enjoy serving the LORD,
and he will give you what you want.'
(Psalm 37:4)

In life, most of us have dreams and goals to aim for. Everyone has at least one talent that God has given to them. It might be playing the piano, being good at football or being artistic. It could be achieving high grades at school or being gifted in communicating. God has given us those talents for a reason.

'We all have different gifts, each of which came because of the grace God gave us ... '
(Romans 12:6)

Prayer

Father God,

Thank you that you know everything about me, and that you have created me the way I am. Thank you that you have given me certain talents for a reason. I pray that you will help me to use them in a way that honours you.

Help me to be individual and happy with the way you made me and help me to hear your voice.

In Jesus' name,

Amen.

An exciting future

' ... From long ago no one
has ever heard of a God like you.
No one has ever seen
a God besides you,
who helps the people who trust you.'
(1 Corinthians 2:9)

God will always be our strongest security and the safest place to be, simply because he is always the same. Things change in our lives all the time but God is constant and will always be unchanging.

It's important to understand that God always wants the best for us. That doesn't mean to say that we won't go through challenging and difficult times, but just knowing that God has plans for us and wants to be involved in our lives can be very helpful when we are struggling in times of doubt and insecurity.

'"I say this because I know what I am planning for you," says the LORD. "I have good plans for you, not plans to hurt you. I will give you hope and a good future."'
(Jeremiah 29:11)

'But God had special plans for me and set me apart for his work even before I was born. He called me through his grace and showed his Son to me so that I might tell the Good News about him ... '
(Galatians 1:15,16)

47 We have a reason to tell people about Jesus!

But what about what I want?

It's really difficult to find a balance between what we want and what God wants. Before I became a Christian, I had a set plan for my future: I wanted to do my A levels, get a good job doing some sort of performing arts, have a nice car, follow in my mum's footsteps and get engaged on my 18th birthday, get married, have two children, and live a successful life with lots of money so I could do whatever I wanted. Yeah right! I very quickly realised that life isn't always like that.

When I became a Christian, it wasn't that God took all that away from me and said I couldn't do it; rather, I loved God and wanted to do things his way. I wanted him to direct my life and tell me what I was doing next because I believed his plans were better than mine. When God created us he gave us free will. He gave us the ability to make decisions and have a choice. So when it says in the Bible that God has plans for our lives, it doesn't mean that he is going to make us do stuff we don't want to do. It means that if we choose to follow his directions he has some good things in store for us.

' ... "We must obey God, not human authority!"'
(Acts 5:29)

Try asking God to reveal to you some of the plans that he has for your life.

In the wilderness

'At three o'clock Jesus cried in a loud voice, "Eli, Eli, lama sabachthani." This means, "My God, my God, why have you rejected me?"'
(Mark 15:34)

You may sometimes face times in your life when you feel lost and lonely, and all you want to do is hide until the time passes. You may feel as though everything is falling apart and no one can even begin to understand what you're going through. Although it may feel like everything is against you, keep going. God hasn't abandoned you and left you to tackle things on your own. He has promised to be with you wherever you go.

' ... because you know that these troubles test your faith, and this will give you patience. Let your patience show itself perfectly in what you do. Then you will be perfect and complete and will have everything you need.'
(James 1:3,4)

Jesus promised this:

'"I will not leave you all alone like orphans ... "'
(John 14:18)

Many Christians, past and present, have talked about being in the wilderness – feeling alone and far from God, but crying out to him desperately for help and comfort. Looking back on their experiences, they have said that it was during those times that their relationship with God really blossomed and they came out of the wilderness with a deeper sense of security and trust in God's love. I remember going through a wilderness experience. It felt like the whole world was against me, and no matter how hard I tried I just couldn't drag myself up. At the time it was horrible. However, looking back, I realise that God was trying to teach me how important it is to depend on him first, before other people.

Go when God says go!

'But you do not know what will happen tomorrow! Your life is like a mist. You can see it for a short time, but then it goes away. So you should say, "If the Lord wants, we will live and do this or that." But now you are proud and you boast. All of this boasting is wrong. Anyone who knows the right thing to do, but does not do it, is sinning.'
(James 4:14-17)

Well, you can't get much clearer than that!

Some time ago, I started asking God to show me what he wanted me to do with my life, as I had a strong sense that I was not on the right track. A few weeks later I received an email from a guy called Chip (Chip K from 'thebandwithnoname') asking me to do an audition in Manchester for a new schools' band that was being set up in Liverpool, by an organisation called 'Innervation'. As soon as I read the email I started jumping around my lounge,

shouting and dancing! My mum and dad couldn't believe it! I knew this was an answer to my prayer about the future.
So I went for the audition and I was the only one out of 15 girls to get the job. And here I am now! I learned so much from that experience, but there were two major things:

Always be obedient to God.

1) No matter what the cost is, always be obedient to God. If you have to leave possessions or people behind, leave them. It will be worth it in the end.

2) Make sure never to miss out on an opportunity that God has put in front of you, because what God has in store for us is always the best thing possible.

Involve God!

It can be really easy when you're faced with a decision, to rely on your own feelings and not to involve God, but we need to involve him in everything, especially when it comes to making decisions. Here are a few ways we can make decisions with God:

- See what it says in the Bible. The Youth Bible has a great section at the front where you can easily look up bits about certain topics.
- Read the 'How do you hear God's voice?' (p44) section again, and try asking God what he thinks you should do. You might be surprised at what he says!
- Seek reliable, Christian advice from someone you look up to, like your minister/pastor, a close friend or a family member.

51

Too young?

'Do not let anyone treat you as if you are unimportant because you are young. Instead, be an example to the believers with your words, your actions, your love, your faith, and your pure life.' (1 Timothy 4:12)

This was an issue I used to really struggle with. I used to think that God couldn't use me because I was too young and that because of my age people wouldn't listen to me. It wasn't until I found myself in a school assembly hall as part of the schools' band, that I realised if God has told you to do it, and equipped you with the right resources, who are you to say you can't? God obviously believed I could do it or he wouldn't have put me in that position.

I found this bit from the Bible a few months ago. At the time, I was going through one of my 'I can't do this' stages, and I desperately needed some encouragement:

'The LORD spoke his word to me, saying:
"Before I made you in your mother's womb,
I chose you.
Before you were born, I set you apart
for a special work.
I appointed you as a prophet to the nations."
Then I said, "But Lord GOD, I don't know how to speak. I am only a boy."
But the LORD said to me, "Don't say, 'I am only a boy.' You must go everywhere I send you, and you must say everything I tell you to say. Don't be afraid

of anyone, because I am with you to protect you," says the LORD.

Then the LORD reached out his hand and touched my mouth. He said to me, "See, I am putting my words in your mouth."'

(Jeremiah 1:4-9)

As soon as I read this, I knew why I was able to do what God has called me to do – because it was part of God's plan for me. It doesn't matter how old you are. We are all children of God.

!

People will often try and stand in your way, but when God says 'go', nothing can stop you!

Prayer

Lord,

Thank you for giving me the freedom to choose.

Thank you that you have good things planned for me.

Help me to depend on you before I depend on other people. Lord, I just want you to know that I love you. I want you to know that I am going to try my best to be obedient and to listen to what you're trying to tell me.

Help me to keep running the race that you have set before me, and to know that when the right time comes to do something, you will tell me.

In Jesus' name,

Amen.

Want to know more...?

One-up

Essential regular help with Bible reading and prayer.

Scripture Union 1360 3051

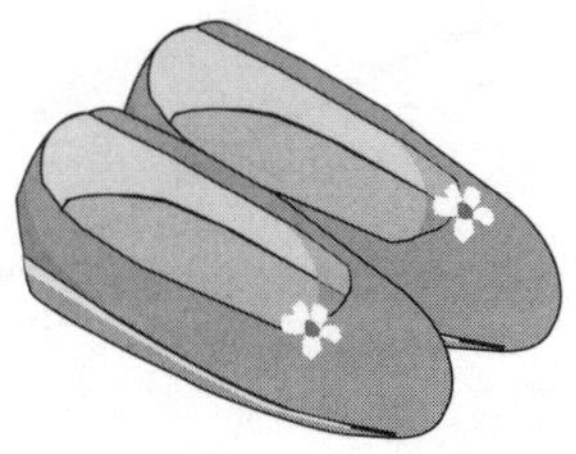

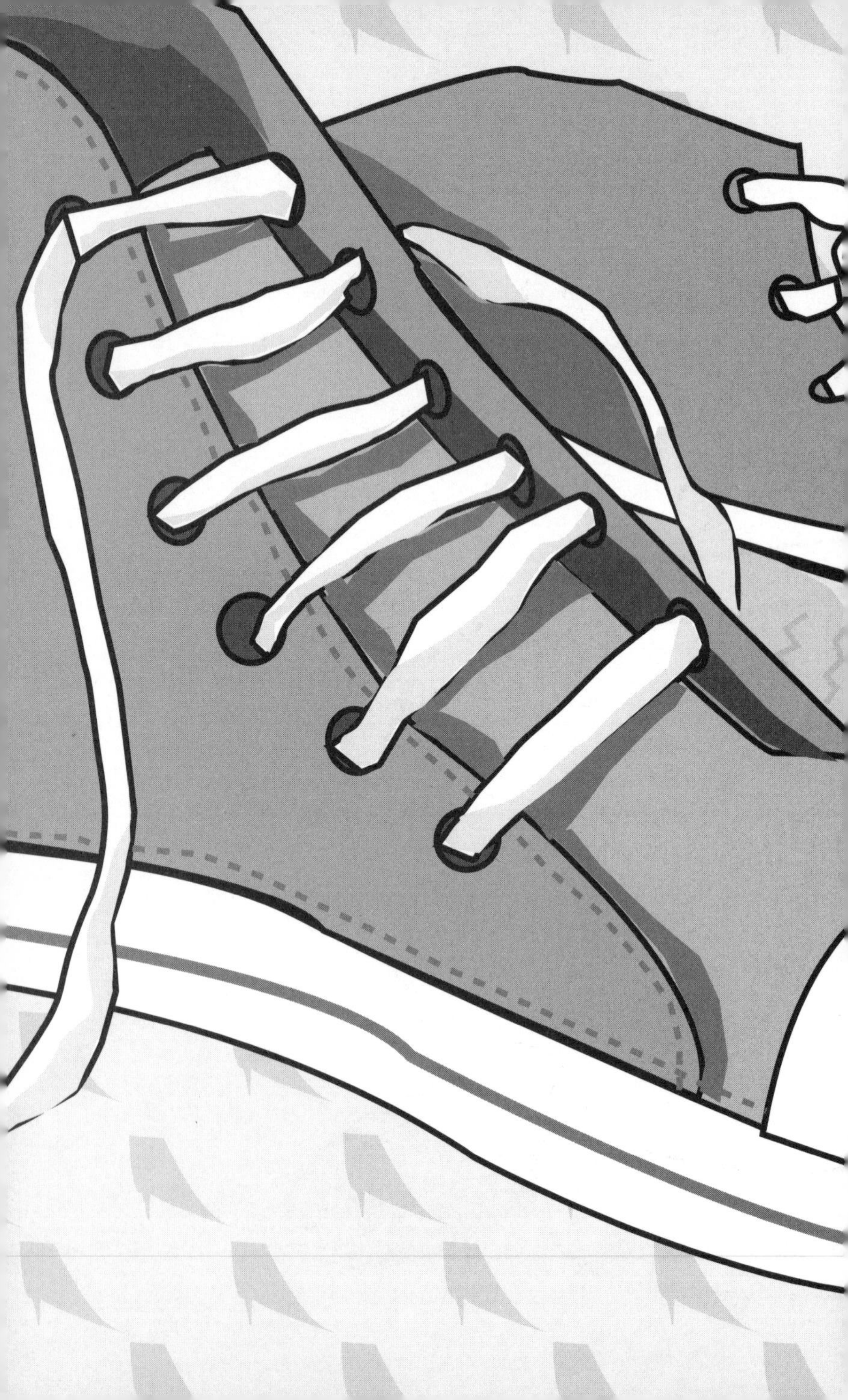

Chapter 4:
Putting your foot in it: Forgiveness and sin

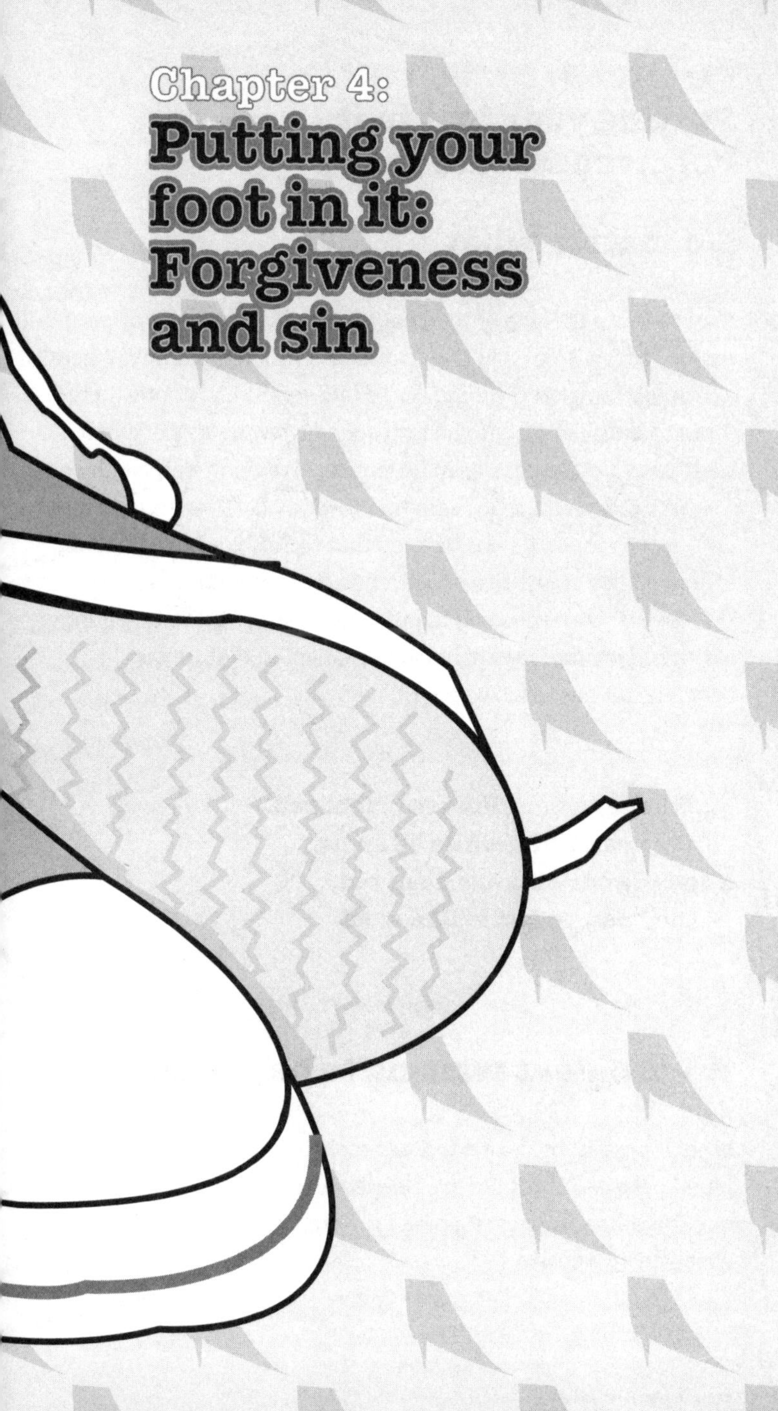

Chapter 4:
Putting your foot in it: Forgiveness and sin

No matter what

I have written the title of this chapter that way round for a specific reason. Why is it not 'Sin and forgiveness'? I'll tell you why. When we sin (do something wrong) God's forgiveness is instantly there for us to grasp hold of. He doesn't spend a few hours working out whether or not we deserve to be forgiven. We don't deserve to be forgiven, but because God sent his one and only son, Jesus, to die on the cross for us, he has restored that friendship with us and we instantly have access to his forgiveness. How awesome is that?! God is more than prepared to put behind him all the wrong things we have done that hurt him and upset him, so that we can continue our friendship with him.

'... Though your sins are bright red,
they can be as white as snow.
Though your sins are deep red,
they can be white like wool.'
(Isaiah 1:18)

An accident waiting to be forgiven

When I passed my driving test with only one minor fault I was so proud of myself. I felt like my independence had reached its peak and there was nothing stopping me from doing exactly what I wanted. Life was good!

I went through four months of driving confidently but, as everyone knows, sometimes being too confident isn't always the best thing. One day, I followed Tim home from work in my own car. However, we didn't manage to get all the way home.

There's a junction near my parents' house that you don't really need to stop at. It's one of those junctions where you can look to see if anything's coming and if there's not, slip into second gear and glide round the corner. So that's exactly what we did. I was driving behind Tim, looking to make sure nothing was coming, and slipped into second gear. The problem was that Tim hadn't moved at all – until I crashed into him and made him go round the corner! There was an almighty bang, smoke everywhere, and two severely injured cars. I immediately broke down in tears and sobbed. In fact, I became hysterical.

I slowly got out and walked over to Tim's car. I knew what was coming. He was going to yell at me and tell me how stupid I was, and how I'd caused so much damage to his car, and it was going to cost a fortune to repair, and it was all my fault for assuming he had driven round the corner.

I immediately cried, 'I'm so sorry!' He looked at my blotchy face, got out of his car, slammed the door shut, firmly placed his arms around me and said, 'I love you.' That was certainly not the reaction I was expecting. Then he continued to say, 'It's all right. We'll get it fixed and we'll sort it out.' That made me cry even more! I couldn't believe that even though I had made such a foolish mistake – the consequences of that mistake resulting in my car being a write-off, Tim's car costing £2,000 to fix, me suffering from whiplash for a week and my insurance premiums increasing by about fifty per cent – Tim was prepared to forgive me. He was prepared to forget all about it and love me just the same.

If there was one thing to learn from my mistake, it was this: Tim acted in exactly the same way that Jesus would have acted. Even though we spend a big chunk of our lives messing up and doing the wrong thing, Jesus forgives us and loves us in return. He died on the cross so that we could be set free, receive a love beyond description and gain instant forgiveness!

Freedom and forgiveness

Repenting is another word used to describe saying sorry. It comes from a Greek word, metanoeo, which means changing one's mind. Being set free from a certain sin is a process:

1) Thought
First of all, we need to realise that what we've done/said/thought is wrong.
2) Word
Second, we need to say sorry. If we admit our sins, the way is open for grace to flow through. Learn to be open and sensitive to God's Spirit.
3) Action
Third, we will feel a longing to turn away from our old ways in order to turn to Jesus and allow him to change us.

'But if we confess our sins, he will forgive our sins, because we can trust God to do what is right. He will cleanse us from all the wrongs we have done.'
(1 John 1:9)

Get rid of the thing that is causing you to sin. This may be costly and time-consuming. It probably won't happen overnight but in the end it will make a difference and be very rewarding.

Grace

'But Lord, you are a God who shows mercy and is kind.
You don't become angry quickly.
You have great love and faithfulness.'
(Psalm 86:15)

Grace is...
God's
Riches
At
Christ's
Expense

The grace that God gives, offers us the ability to be able to resist temptation and overcome sin. I find it so encouraging to know that God has given me the strength to turn away from sin. Therefore, there is no excuse for me holding on to sin in my life.

'For our high priest is able to understand our weaknesses. When he lived on earth, he was tempted in every way that we are, but he did not sin. Let us, then, feel very sure that we can come before God's throne where there is grace. There we can receive mercy and grace to help us when we need it.'
(Hebrews 4:15,16)

'He has not punished us as our sins should be punished;
he has not repaid us for the evil we have done.'
(Psalm 103:10)

How can God love me?

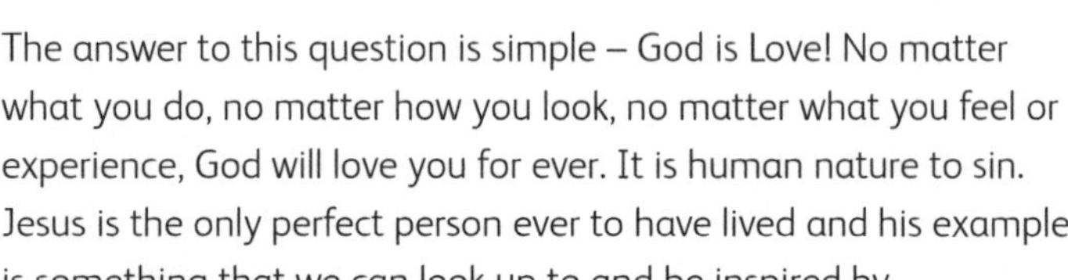

God is Love!

The answer to this question is simple – God is Love! No matter what you do, no matter how you look, no matter what you feel or experience, God will love you for ever. It is human nature to sin. Jesus is the only perfect person ever to have lived and his example is something that we can look up to and be inspired by.

When I first became a Christian, I was so frightened of doing things wrong. I got myself in such a mess about it and I would feel really guilty and ashamed. I spoke about it to my mentor (an older Christian friend – I talk more about mentors in Chapter 5) and she said that God was not a God of blame and guilt, but a God of love and forgiveness, and that it was okay to be sorry for what I'd done wrong, but to know that God had already forgiven me and had enabled me to move on. As soon as I heard that, it felt like I was walking my way back down that path of freedom that Jesus had put in front of me.

I began to realise how easy it is to be distracted from what God has planned for us. We can end up focusing on our weaknesses and failures, and being sidetracked from Jesus' everlasting promise of forgiveness.

Jesus and the sinful woman

Try to imagine that you're in the scene as you read this Bible story.

'One of the Pharisees asked Jesus to eat with him, so Jesus went into the Pharisee's house and sat at the table. A sinful woman in the town learnt that Jesus was eating at the Pharisee's house. So she brought an alabaster jar of perfume and stood behind Jesus at his feet, crying. She began to wash his feet with her tears, and she dried them with her hair, kissing them many times and rubbing them with the perfume.'
(Luke 7:36-38)

Just picture that. You're sat down having dinner with a VIP, when in runs a woman with a bottle of perfume. She climbs under the table and starts washing Jesus' feet in front of everyone. She's hysterically crying out loud and wiping his feet with her hair. I don't know about you, but I would think she was crazy! But that's where Jesus is different. He sees her heart.

'When the Pharisee who asked Jesus to come to his house saw this, he thought to himself, "If Jesus were a prophet, he would know that the woman touching him is a sinner!"'
(Luke 7:39)

Sometimes it can be so easy for us to judge other people by their actions and words. However, Jesus deals with the situation very differently. (Read the rest of the story in Luke 7:36-50.)

This story shows the true character of Jesus. Simon, the Pharisee, was quick to judge the woman even though he was a sinner himself. Jesus knew the woman's heart and knew how much she had done wrong, but still loved her. He still forgave her. He still accepted her worship.

This passage also highlights the fact that we will never be in a position to repay Jesus for all that he has done so freely for us. We will never be able to understand the pain and suffering he went through on the cross. We will never fully recognise the value of our undeserved forgiveness, but in some ways that doesn't matter. Jesus just wants to give us all that he has for us. He loves us and he died to forgive us. So it doesn't matter what you've done wrong in the past. Just know that Jesus wants to concentrate on your future and that if you've repented, you've already been forgiven for everything you have ever done wrong. It's a fact!

Turning away from temptation

'But you, man of God ... '

(1 Timothy 6:11)

Temptation is an aspect of life that is a constant battle. However, there are ways of knowing how to deal with it so that it doesn't become a problem for us.

First of all, we need to learn how to recognise it. For instance, when you log on to the internet to check your emails and find an email address you don't recognise, but the title of the email is, 'Find your BIG BOY today', it isn't going to be an email from a friend, is it? It's not going to be helpful for your mind or for your heart. So in circumstances like that one, use your common sense, and the gift of self-control that God has blessed you with, and delete it straight away.

Another example might be to do with one of your friends. I remember when I had a huge argument with my mum because she'd said something that I had taken in the wrong way. We argued about it for ages until I realised that she didn't mean what she had said. She meant for it to come out differently.

In any similar situation, it's tempting to get defensive and stick up for yourself. However, God has given you the ability to have grace for each other, take a step back from the situation and just to let it go. It's easy when you think about it but when you're actually in the heat of the moment, it's an extremely difficult thing to do.

Remember: you belong to God.

'But you, man of God, run away from all those things. Instead, live in the right way, serve God, have faith, love, patience and gentleness.
(1 Timothy 6:11)

Every single one of us has given in to temptation at some point in our lives. All of us have fallen short of God's pure and holy ways. However, God, by his grace, can help us overcome temptation. He knows we can't do it on our own.

Prayer
Lord,

Thank you that you have given me grace to enable me to walk away from temptation and that even when

I mess up you still love me just the way I am.

Help me to resist temptation. Thank you that you're more powerful than any temptation I face. Please help me to be strong.

In the name of your holy and precious Son, Amen.

The power of prayer

'... When a believing person prays, great things happen.'
(James 5:16)

A while ago, I needed a new pair of trainers for dancing but I couldn't afford them. So I prayed. I asked God to provide me, in some way, with a pair of trainers. A few days went by and then I received an email from a friend in Holland. At the end of the email, he said that I should tell him if there was anything I really needed and he would get it for me. It didn't matter how expensive it was because he would pay for it. I was shocked! I sent an email back telling him that I needed a new pair of trainers for dancing. Two weeks later I received a cheque from him for £60 and I was able to buy some new trainers. How awesome is that? God totally answered my prayer!

Prayer is an essential part of having a relationship with God. He wants us to communicate our needs to him and speak to him, just as we would communicate our needs to anyone else. However, prayer isn't just about asking God for material things we need or would like (he already knows). He wants us to communicate with him. Through prayer we can tell him how amazing he is and give him our praise. We can cry out to him when we're feeling down and lonely. We can ask for things for ourselves and for other people. Praying simply means talking to God as a friend.

Try keeping a prayer diary and write down all of your praise and prayers, favourite Bible verses and songs. Prayer diaries are useful for when you want to look back at what God has done in your life. Turn to page 112 to find out about a fantastic prayer journal that you might like to buy and use to help you.

Ask and you will receive

'And this is the boldness we have in God's presence: that if we ask God for anything that agrees with what he wants, he hears us. If we know he hears us every time we ask him, we know we have what we ask from him.'
(1 John 5:14,15)

When I became a Christian, I made the mistake of doubting God's power and faithfulness. I would pray to God and ask him for things but never really believed that God was going to answer my prayer. There was always a certain amount of doubt in my mind. It wasn't until I experienced the power of God and he answered my prayer that I believed he could do it.

Whenever TBC are in a school taking lessons, we always have a question time at the end of the lesson, and people often seem to have confused ideas about what prayer is. There were a number of boys once who asked, 'If I pray to God tonight that Liverpool will win the footy match tomorrow, does that mean they will win?'

Can you imagine what the world would be like if God said yes to everything we asked for? You would never have to do any homework, teachers would accept the excuse of 'I haven't got my schoolbook with me because the dog ate it last night', and every girl in the world would have the most gorgeous boyfriend ever! No one would ever suffer or die, and we would always get exactly what we wanted. The world would be in a bigger mess than it is now. What we ask for might not be the best thing for us. We may think it is at the time, but there may actually be something better for us just around the corner. I'm glad that God can see the bigger picture.

'But when you ask God, you must believe and not doubt. Anyone who doubts is like a wave in the sea, blown up and down by the wind.'

(James 1:6)

It can be disheartening when we ask God for something and it doesn't happen, especially when our prayers are about someone who is suffering in some way. It's in these situations that we have to trust in God even more. For example, having anorexia was one of the hardest times of my life so far. I really struggled to deal with it and I had to keep fighting to get through it. However, God has used my experience to help other people and in turn bring glory to him. God has the ability to use everything for good.

When you don't get what you want, there's usually a pretty good reason for it. Maybe God doesn't want you to have something because it's dangerous, or maybe it's just not the right time. Maybe God will answer your prayer, just not in the way you wanted him to. But be assured that God wants the best for you.

'... your Father knows the things you need before you ask him.'

(Matthew 6:8)

When to pray

There isn't a set answer to this issue. It really depends on you and your routine. I know a lot of people who get up half an hour earlier in the morning to pray and have a quiet time with God. But I am definitely not a morning person, so that wouldn't really suit me. Some people do it last thing at night, but the danger with that is falling asleep in the middle of a prayer! I tend to do it when I get home from work. I'll just grab a cup of tea and go up to my room on my own and read my Bible for however long I need. Sometimes it's ten minutes, sometimes it's an hour. There's no right or wrong answer.

We can pray any time, anywhere and have access to God.

In terms of how much you should pray, God didn't write a section in the Bible that said 'you must pray for half an hour on Monday, all day on Wednesday, for ten minutes at twelve o'clock on Thursday...' I try to have a quiet time every day. Some people have more and some have less. It's completely up to you. I would suggest that you try to get into some kind of routine and then do your best to stick to it. The truth is though, that we can pray any time, anywhere and have access to God 24/7!

'Pray in the Spirit at all times with all kinds of prayers, asking for everything you need. To do this you must always be ready and never give up. Always pray for all God's people.'
(Ephesians 6:18)

Worship

'Don't worship any other god, because I, the LORD, the Jealous One, am a jealous God.'
(Exodus 34:14)

How awesome is it to know that God is so passionate about his relationship with us? When you think about the things he has done for us, he deserves our worship because he is not only our God, but also our best friend and our Father.

There are so many different ways to worship God – reading the Bible, praying, singing worshipful songs, working, serving, telling people about Jesus etc. I'm sure I've missed loads out. People have different styles of worship too. For example, some people like to worship God by singing hymns, whereas other people like to worship him by singing pop songs. The best thing about it is that God accepts all worship. It's not about whether or not we can sing, or whether we choose to worship God by singing, praising him or writing. It's about the quality of our heart. Remember, life is an act of worship.

Finding the right church

When I moved to Liverpool, I found it really difficult to find a church that was what I wanted. Some churches were too big and some were too small. Some churches preferred to sing a bit more, and others preferred to pray a bit more. Some churches met together in a traditional building and some met in a modern one.

It can be a nightmare trying to find a church that suits your needs. The best bit of advice I can give you is, take your time. There's no rush. It's so important that you are part of a church where you feel comfortable. Going to church can be exciting and it's a place where you meet other people who believe the same things as you. When you find the right church, you'll know. You'll feel like you belong there and you'll want to start getting involved. And don't forget that there will be a church that actually needs you! If you can sing or play an instrument, they might need you to be part of a worship band; if you're good at reading, they might need you to read the Bible out loud once in a while; if you're good at making cups of tea, they might need you to serve tea and coffee after the service. There are loads of things you could take part in within a church.

How can you get involved?

I suggest that the first thing you do is find a church that God is calling you to be part of, and enjoy being in the church family for a while. Then you can start thinking about how you might get involved. There are so many areas of church service that you can join in with. You may be talented in singing or worship leading and there may be an opportunity for you to shadow a worship leader for a while, or get involved with some all-age worship. You may want to be part of the welcome team or you may have a servant heart and be interested in providing tea and coffee at the end of the service. Maybe you have a heart for working with the children/youth and you could ask to shadow a youth leader. Try different things and explore different areas. Don't worry if it takes you a while to find something that you can really get involved with. Just keep going!

A word of encouragement

God has done so many wonderful things in my life that it's difficult to know where to start, but I just want to share one of them with you, to encourage you.

I write a lot of my own songs and I felt that God gave me a dream to record an album of my own songs. So I got in touch with a Christian recording studio and started to plan how to do it. We planned everything from the songs I wanted on the album to the photograph for the front cover. It was going to cost approximately £400 per track and that meant I had to raise £4,000. So I started praying for the money and asking God to provide it.

This went on for a while and I was persistent in my prayers. Later on in the year, I sang at an event at a park in Warrington with my school. The following week, I walked into the hairdressers and sat down on the chair, waiting for a stylist. Then this man I had never met before, span round on his chair as he was having his hair cut and shouted,

'You're that girl who was singing at the park on Sunday. I thought you were fantastic!'

As you can imagine, I was quite surprised but thanked him. We had a brief chat and that was it. The week after that I was asked to sing at a YFC partners' meal. I set my equipment up, did a quick soundcheck and then went to mingle with the crowd. As I went round chatting, to my complete surprise, guess what? I saw the same man who had seen me at the park and who I'd met in the hairdressers. I couldn't believe it!

To cut a long story short, this man really felt that God was telling him to give me some money for the first track of my album. That proves that God works in all sorts of amazing ways.

Prayer

Lord,

Thank you so much that no matter what I do wrong or how many times I hurt you, you're prepared to forgive me. Thank you that I am able to walk a path of freedom and that you will lead the way.

Lord, help me to know your forgiveness for me. Help me to praise you in every situation. Help me to worship you the way you deserve to be worshipped. I pray that you will help me find the right church, and if I am already in the right church, show me how to get more involved.

I love you Lord,

Amen.

Want to know more...?

You and God: The essential prayer diary *Elaine Carr*

With space to write your own thoughts and prayers this is a brilliant way to get talking to God regularly.

Scripture Union 1 84427 025 4

Connecting to God *Dave Gatward*

Bite-size prayer ideas for those two-minute moments.

Scripture Union 1 85999 759 7

In these shoes?!

Chapter 5:

Footloose and fancy-free: Relationships

Chapter 5:
Footloose and fancy-free: Relationships

Be like Jesus

The entire world revolves around relationships. Whether it's the relationship between you and your parents, you and your boyfriend, you and your best friend or simply between you and your pet hamster, it's a relationship. All relationships take time and effort in order to be successful. However, there is a potential danger in any relationship that we can get things wrong, or that Satan can attempt to mess them up.

Have you ever been in a situation where someone says something to you and you don't know quite how to take it? Are they making a compliment or simply hacking away at your confidence? Suddenly those few words may become the cause of a discussion, which then turns into an argument, which then escalates into anger – and before you know it, that person no longer plays a part in your life because you can't resolve your differences. All because a few words weren't explained properly and neither one of you had the guts to say sorry.

'A gentle answer will calm a person's anger, but an unkind answer will cause more anger.'
(Proverbs 15:1)

There's a way to succeed in any relationship – be like Jesus! Jesus was the master when it came to relationships. He had the key to success. When people were against him, he seemed to know exactly the right words to say. When people misbehaved, he knew exactly how to deal with them. When people were hurting, he knew exactly how to meet their needs. Do you wish that sometimes you were like that – that in every relationship and conversation, you knew how to act in exactly the right way? Well, the good thing is that if we stick to the commands Jesus has given us, we can.

'I give you a new command: love each other. You must love each other as I have loved you.'
(John 13:34)

Jesus loves you no matter what.

One of the hardest but best things you can do, is love someone even when they have hurt you or let you down. It is through these times that we have to be secure and know that Jesus loves us, no matter what.

My car got broken into a few years ago, outside my house. All my CDs were gone and the contents of my glovebox were scattered all over the floor. My door had been bent, the upholstery was scarred and I was really upset. I reported it to the police and then sat down to think. I felt so angry that someone had broken into my car, vandalised my property, stolen my CDs and had got away with it. However, as hard as it may be, God commands us to love our enemies and I knew I had to forgive them, even though they had caused me so much trouble and expense. It was very difficult but it was something I knew I had to do.

'Jesus answered, "'Love the Lord your God with all your heart, all your soul and all your mind.' This is the first and most important command. And the second command is like the first: 'Love your neighbour as you love yourself.' All the law and the writings of the prophets depend on these two commands."'

(Matthew 22:37-40)

Jesus knows what it's like to go through times when you feel like giving up (he was tempted in the wilderness). He knows what it is like to be let down by people you love (his disciples deserted him at Gethsemane; Peter denied him). He knows what it's like to lose someone special and be upset about it (he wept at Lazarus' tomb). However, Jesus is the only person who can truly comfort us and give us what we need to get through life's storms. When you go through hard times in your relationships, remember that God loves you unconditionally and is always there for you. The amazing thing is that just knowing this will help you to love other people.

Who surrounds you?

I once heard someone say that there are two things that make a difference to being who you are – the books you read, and the people you hang out with. When you think about it, it's very true. I read the Bible, which obviously has a massive impact on my life, and I try to surround myself with some good Christian friends. These two aspects of my life are what feed my soul and make me who I am today. If I changed my friends and stopped reading the Bible, I'm guessing that it would change my life quite a lot.

'Don't make friends with bad-tempered people
or spend time with those who have bad tempers.
If you do, you will be like them.
Then you will be in real danger.

(Proverbs 22:24,25)

If the majority of your friends aren't as mature as you, or haven't got a great relationship with God, the chances are you will spend most of your time trying desperately to build them up and help them to grow in their faith. At the time, it may seem like the right thing to do, but after a while it becomes draining and emotionally tiring. That's not to say that you shouldn't encourage your friends, but if you're not getting anything back, you need to start asking some questions. Relationships are two-way things. They require giving from both sides. However, if your friends are people you look up to, and people you feel happy going to for advice because you know they will tell it to you straight, you will undoubtedly grow and mature as a Christian and be able to pass that advice on to others.

Every person who is ever in your life will leave some kind of trace.

Someone once said to me that you only have a few spaces for close friends in your life and if you try to fill them up with too many people you will end up being half-hearted in your friendships. Although some people will be a part of your life for a while, very few people will play a part in it for a lifetime. You may be sitting there right now trying to imagine which of your friends will be there in twenty years' time, but the truth is, you can't possibly say.

> **'I no longer call you servants, because a servant does not know what his master is doing. But I call you friends, because I have made known to you everything I heard from my Father.'**
> (John 15:15)

Jesus is the only friend you can ever count on to be there through thick and thin. He will be there for a lifetime, no matter what. We are so privileged to be called God's friends when we don't deserve to be, but he loves us that much.

Having a mentor

When I became a Christian, my youth leader suggested that it would be a good idea to have a mentor. I didn't have a clue what he was going on about! A mentor is someone (usually of the same sex as you) who spends quality time with you. They can help you through things, encourage you in your relationship with God, give you wise advice and be just a mate! A mentor is usually someone who is older than you, just because they will then have experienced more things than you, and perhaps have gone through similar things that you are going through.

I used to meet with my mentor once a week. We would usually chat about what had happened in the time since our last meeting. That would then lead us into conversation about various issues and topics. Sometimes, my mentor would prepare a Bible-study for us to do, sometimes we would go out for coffee and sometimes we would just sit and chill out together. Normally, we would end our time together by praying.

A mentor is someone you can be accountable to. Whether you do things right or wrong, you can tell them and they will support you in it. It can take a while to get to a stage where your mentor knows everything about you but all friendships take time and effort.

If you think having a mentor would be a good idea, why don't you have a chat about it with your youth leader or someone from your church? They may know the best thing to do and who to put you in contact with. Make sure it's someone you have something in common with and who you fully respect.

Prayer

Lord,

Thank you that you want to be my best friend. Thank you for all the people that you have placed in my life whether it's for a reason, a season or a lifetime. Help me to use the time I have with those people in the way you want me to.

Help me to surround myself with the right people. Help me to have friends I can encourage, and who encourage and support me too. Help me to be more and more like you.

In Jesus' name,

Amen.

Just another fish in the sea?

I remember when I was a little girl I used to lie in bed at night and wonder what my Prince Charming would look like. I always imagined him to be a stereotypical tall, dark and handsome man, with a good dress sense, and he'd be absolutely loaded! I used to wonder what it would be like to be swept off my feet like a princess, and made to feel like I was the most important girl in the world. My dream man would buy me presents all the time, like flowers and chocolates. He'd take me out for expensive dinners in big, posh restaurants and at the click of a finger, the waiter would come and pour another glass of sparkling champagne. After that, he would take me home and passionately kiss me on the front step of my house, like they do in the movies, and then drive off leaving me all warm and bubbly inside.

If any of you have ever had a boyfriend, you're probably thinking, 'Yeah, right!' If you have never had a boyfriend, you may be clinging to the dream that you will be the one girl in the world to find a man exactly like that!

!

God wants the best for us.

Most of us will have an expectation, or a very good idea, of what we want our man to be like, look like, act like, take after – but this can sometimes lead to the wrong person. You may want your boyfriend to look like Brad Pitt and one day you're walking down the street and you coincidentally walk into someone who looks exactly like him. Your heart skips a beat and you're already thinking about marriage and having babies and them being the best-looking babies on this planet! He asks you out for a coffee and you hit it off straight away. You go out on a few dates but on your third time out with this guy, you realise he's not the person you expected him to be. You discover all of his annoying habits, like he is always text messaging people on his mobile, even when he's in the middle of a conversation with you, and he always expects you to buy the drinks because he's just run out of cash. But worst of all, you find out that he is a chain-smoker with really bad breath and he absolutely stinks! Suddenly, you know that you couldn't have a meaningful relationship with a man like that, and realise that it's time to ditch him while you can!

Obviously, not all relationships start and finish in such a dramatic way, but that's just a little illustration to make you aware of these things.

I tend to ask myself five questions:

Is he a Christian?
Do I feel I can be myself with him?
Does he feel he can be himself with me?
Do I trust him to respect me and my values?
Do we have fun together?

If the answer is yes to all these questions and you've prayed about it, then go for it and see how it goes. If the answer is no to even one of these questions, then I would advise you to be very careful in making your decision. I found the questions very helpful when I was deciding about whether or not to go out with Tim.

Relationships take time. Trust and commitment take time to build up, and the whole area of what each person expects from the relationship has to be tackled with honesty and integrity. There are some great books about teenage dating. See the list at the end of this chapter for tips on how to cope with the dating scene.

The 'S' word

The number of times I have heard Christians being referred to as 'people who aren't allowed to have sex' is unbelievable! Of course Christians are allowed to have sex. It's just that God gave it to us as a gift to give to another person and he wants us to keep it for 'the one'.

'So a man will leave his father and mother and be united with his wife, and the two will become one body. So there are not two, but one. God has joined the two together, so no one should separate them.'
(Mark 10:7,8)

God didn't make sex a thing for marriage just so that we would get frustrated and impatient beforehand. He did it so that we would be protected. I know you're probably thinking, 'What are you going on about?' Let me explain.

No matter what anyone says, sex is an extremely intimate thing and it creates an unbreakable bond between you and your partner. One of my friends slept with their partner before they were married. At the time, it felt like the right thing to do. It seemed the best way to show the other person the feelings they had for them. Some time later, they split up and they were both left with the baggage of having had sex with someone other than their wife or husband of the future. At some point they were going to have to tell the person they were going to marry what had happened in their previous relationship and they knew it was going to hurt.

Believe it or not, when God decided to make sex a thing for marriage, he did it with our best interests at heart. He knows that if you have a sexual relationship with someone, you are opening up your whole self to them – not only physically, but also emotionally and spiritually (whether you admit it or not). This is great when you are married to Mr Right. However, if the sexual relationship is not within the context of a loving, committed marriage, you are making yourself extremely vulnerable. This is particularly crucial for girls, who are often more emotionally sensitive than boys and may end up suffering the consequences (emotional hurt if the relationship breaks up, guilt, higher risk of cervical cancer if you are a young teenager, teenage pregnancy and single parenthood…). Sexually transmitted diseases are becoming more and more common amongst people these days. Let me bore you with a few facts!

- The majority of people with AIDS are infected between the ages of 15 and 24. (And that is not to say that people outside of that age bracket won't be affected!)
- Condoms are not 100 per cent effective in preventing STDs or pregnancy.
- Only 14 per cent of teenage relationships last more than a year. So even when you think you've found Mr Right, the chances are you'll be waiting a few years for the right one. Sorry to disappoint you!

I know it sounds drastic but it's totally true. God is concerned about you and your future and he doesn't want you to make a mistake that could potentially ruin friendships and relationships later on in life.

How to deal with it all

'So, do not let sin control your life here on earth so that you do what your sinful self wants to do. Do not offer the parts of your body to serve sin, as things to be used in doing evil. Instead, offer yourselves to God as people who have died and now live. Offer the parts of your body to God to be used in doing good. Sin will not be your master, because you are not under law but under God's grace.'

(Romans 6:12-14)

God has already given us everything we need to live a fulfilling life that glorifies him. He has also given us the ability to fight off desires for sex and to use our bodies worshipfully for him. It is important to remember this, particularly when today's media bombards us with messages that looking sexy and having sex is the main reason for living. It's difficult enough for us girls to maintain our sense of self-esteem without that pressure!

!

You need to walk away!

It can be difficult to fight off desires for sex when you're in the moment – when your heart's beating fast and your legs feel like jelly. However, there are ways of coping. One of the best ways is not to allow yourself to get into a risky situation in the first place. First, decide in advance that you definitely don't want to have sex if you are not in a committed marriage relationship, for all of the above reasons. Talk over your decision with older, trustworthy Christian friends and ask for their encouragement and support in your decision. Pray for God's help and strength to stick to your decision, no matter what. Read helpful Christian books and magazines on dating as a teenager (see the end of this chapter for some suggestions). Think about how far you'd feel comfortable with going physically, should you be in a relationship with someone you are attracted to. If you start going out with someone, talk over your decision with him and make sure he fully respects (and preferably shares) your views. If you are both Christians and feel comfortable praying together about the whole issue of self-control, this may be helpful. Think clearly about what you do and the places you go to when you meet up; it may be more helpful to have your first few dates in places where other people will be around (cafes, restaurants, cinema etc), or go out in groups of friends, to dilute any intensity of feeling. Sometimes it's harder for boys to be as self-controlled as girls, so you may have to think honestly about the body language you are using when you are around your boyfriend, the clothes you are wearing and so on.

Nevertheless, it is very normal to have these strong feelings of attraction and despite all your safety checks, you may still end up feeling in the moment and unable or unwilling to stop. But that's when it is crucial to do something about it. Learn to get out of the moment! It's not going to be any help for either of you if you just sit there and let time pass, twiddling your thumbs as you think about what could've happened. You need to walk away. When Potiphar's wife was begging Joseph to have sex with her, do you really think Joseph sat there and said, 'Now I'm not going to have sex with you, but we can just sit here and chat?' No! He ran as far away from the moment as he possibly could! Start acting responsibly about your body and sexuality now, and you won't regret it later on in life.

Where to draw the line

Unfortunately, the Bible doesn't say anything about where to draw the line. The whole teenage dating scene wasn't really an issue in biblical times; it just says that you shouldn't have sex. People take this in different ways. Some people say that it's okay to do anything physical in your relationship as long as you don't actually have sex. Other people think that even kissing and holding hands is inappropriate. However, there are some common sense guidelines which you're probably familiar with: don't lie down together; don't touch anything you don't have yourself; don't undo or take off clothes; avoid being alone together in an empty house/secluded place; recognise when you're getting too turned on and stop, etc. There may seem a lot of negatives here, but it is important to remember that there is a very valuable reason for waiting until you are married, and have freedom to express yourself sexually within a lifetime commitment. In the meantime, have fun dating. Enjoy spending time with each other; find out about each other (similarities and differences, good points and bad points); respect each other's values; grow as a Christian within a caring, honest relationship. No relationship can be based only on sex. It has to be based on love, trust and all the other necessary ingredients a relationship needs to be successful.

What happens if I've had sex before marriage?

Like any other sin on the planet, if you say sorry to God and truly repent of it, he will forgive you. However, the hardest thing to be released from is the emotional and spiritual bond that has been created between you and your ex-partner. This can sometimes take a long time and be a massive emotional trek, but by the end of it you will feel free and restored. There's no easy answer to when it will be sorted by, but when it finally is, in your heart you will know.

It may affect relationships in the future and that will inevitably be difficult for you, but when someone loves you, they love you for your past, present and future. If he is the right one for you, you will get over it together and your wedding night will be the most special night of your life!

What if you're still sleeping with someone and are feeling uncomfortable with the situation, but don't know what to do about it? (Maybe it was an accident the first time, and it seems too late to put the clock back, or maybe you felt pressurised by your boyfriend, or by your non-Christian friends?) Pray about your feelings and the situation, and ask God to help you through it; talk to an older Christian friend whom you trust; read some of the helpful books on this area (see p89).

As I was saying in chapter 4, God offers every single one of us forgiveness for the stuff we've done wrong if we're really sorry. Whatever situation you may be in at the moment, know that God wants to help you and his hand is already there to grab hold of. But you have to make the decision for yourself. God is there for you every minute of every day – make the most of it!

It's important to understand that not everyone has to get married. Some people prefer not to get married until they are a lot older, some people don't want to ever get married and some people may want to get married but never find a partner. I got married when I was 20, which some people think is quite young, but I was ready to make that step. It's between you and God, and it's about what's right for you personally. Don't ever feel that you have to get married or that you have to find Mr Right before you are 30 or 40 or 50! Just do what you feel is right for you.

Prayer

Lord,

Thank you that you have got our best interests at heart and that you have created sex as a physical act of love to take place in a marriage relationship. Thank you that even if I have messed up, you are prepared to forgive and forget.

Help me to understand your ways when it comes to relationships. Help me to have self-control in my relationship with my boyfriend now, or any boyfriend I may have in the future, and help me to know where to draw the line when it comes to physical boundaries.

I'm sorry for all the things that I've done wrong within relationships in the past. Help me to move on and receive your true forgiveness.

I love you Lord Jesus,

Amen

Want to know more...?

Friends First *Claire Pedrick + Andy Morgan*

Boyfriends, best-friends, even being friends with your parents?! The ultimate guide to relationships.

Scripture Union 1 85999 644 2

Chapter 6:
Putting your best foot forward: Trust and obedience

Chapter 6:
Putting your best foot forward: Trust and obedience

Learning to trust

It is hard to have total trust in another person but it really helps to know that we can trust God absolutely (more about that later on in this chapter). It may be easy to trust the people you know and love with small things. However, when you find yourself having to trust someone with something much bigger, you can quickly find yourself running scared.

I used to have a massive problem with trust. As I was growing up I found it so difficult to trust my friends. It felt like as soon as I had developed some sort of trust with them, they started talking about me behind my back and spreading stupid rumours. Some things can happen again and again and will never affect you, whereas trust only has to be broken once for you to find it difficult to trust people again.

As I got older, trust became even harder for me to deal with. I had a big problem when it came to trusting boys. As a teenager, boys were attracted to me in a physical way. They would pass me as I was walking down the street and shout sexual comments at me. At college everyone knew that I was a Christian and that I didn't believe in having sex before marriage, but all they seemed to be interested in was who could have sex with me first, because they thought it would be an achievement to be the first person to sleep with me. Many women would take that as a compliment but I hated it more than anything else. All through my life I have seemed to get on better with boys than girls. So I would meet a boy, become friends with them and everything would be cool. Then after a few months or so, they would normally turn round and say that they fancied me and wanted something more than a friendship. This, as you can probably imagine, ruined the friendship and I was always left with nothing. As the years passed by, it seemed to happen more and more. It was as though every friendship I had was destroyed because the other person was never satisfied with just being my friend. I found myself being afraid of boys because I always ended up feeling hurt after being around them. The trust I had towards boys had been shattered.

As God has brought me into a new chapter of my life, I have started to deal with these issues and realise that you can have friends that are boys and have a normal friendship.

'Let us hold firmly to the hope that we have confessed, because we can trust God to do what he promised.'
(Hebrews 10:23)

Obedience

We may tend to associate the word 'obedience' with negative things (rules, regulations, the law, being told off, doing things wrong, etc). However, when we're talking about God, obedience – although it may be difficult – leads to having true fulfilment.

' ... It is better to obey than to sacrifice ... '
(1 Samuel 15:22)

'... What pleases the LORD more:
burnt offerings and sacrifices
or obedience to his voice?
It is better to obey than to sacrifice ... '
(1 Samuel 15:22)

Wing it!

I am constantly amazed at what can happen when we allow God to intervene and are obedient to his direction. However, as a society we like to be in control of our own destiny. We hate the thought of losing control and winging it. However, in the Old Testament, there are inspirational examples of brave individuals who were prepared to have incredible faith in God and wing it, with amazing results.

God recently challenged me through a Bible scripture from Genesis 22.

'After these things God tested Abraham's faith. God said to him, "Abraham!"

And he answered, "Here I am."

Then God said, "Take your only son, Isaac, the son you love, and go to the land of Moriah. Kill him there and offer him as a whole burnt offering on one of the mountains I will tell you about."
(Genesis 22:1,2)

The amount of trust and faith that Abraham had in God was massive. Try to put yourself in Abraham's shoes: he had waited patiently for many years for the son that he and Sarah so desperately wanted. But when God eventually blessed them with a child, he told Abraham to go and sacrifice him. The next bit amazes me even more! Without question, Abraham went to do what God had told him to do. He didn't sit there and have a little argument with God until he changed his mind. He just went. No questions, no fuss, nothing. As Abraham prepared to sacrifice Isaac, a strange thing happened.

'But the angel of the LORD called to him from heaven and said, "Abraham! Abraham!"

Abraham answered, "Yes."

The angel said, "Don't kill your son or hurt him in any way. Now I can see that you trust God and that you have not kept your son, your only son, from me."

Then Abraham looked up and saw a ram caught in a bush by its horns. So Abraham went and took the ram and killed it. He offered it as a whole burnt offering to God, and his son was saved. So Abraham named that place The LORD Provides. Even today people say, "On the mountain of the LORD it will be provided."'

(Genesis 22:11-14)

God then knew that Abraham was prepared to obey him and follow his commands to any extent, in spite of the cost. In the final part of this passage, we begin to understand why God asked Abraham to fulfil such a horrific task:

'The angel of the LORD called to Abraham from heaven a second time and said, "The LORD says,

'Because you did not keep back your son, your only son, from me, I make you this promise by my own name: I will surely bless you and give you many descendants ... all the nations on the earth will be blessed, because you obeyed me.'"'
(Genesis 22:15-18)

' ... All the nations on the earth will be blessed, because you obeyed me.'
(Genesis 22:18)

Wow! What a promise! God had to know 110 per cent that Abraham was willing to give up anything and everything in order to be used by him. His massive step of obedience was a real inspiration to later generations.

'You belong to Christ, so you are Abraham's descendants. You will inherit all of God's blessings because of the promise God made to Abraham.'
(Galatians 3:29)

Sacrifice

Before I became part of 'tbc' God made it clear that he wanted me to make the biggest sacrifice in my life so far – my relationship with Tim. At that point, Tim and I had been going out for nearly a year and a half. We were so happy together. I couldn't understand why God was asking me to do this, but deep down inside I knew I had to be obedient to his call, no matter how hard it was going to be.

As soon as I told Tim, he was shocked and upset. I felt terrible for hurting him so much and I just hoped God knew what he was doing. Tim went home and we left each other feeling alone and miserable.

About a week later, Tim and I happened to be at the same church service. The preacher asked everyone to turn to Genesis 22. He read out the whole passage about Abraham being asked to sacrifice his son and what happened after that. At the same time, both Tim and I related what was going on in our relationship to what was happening in Genesis 22. God had wanted us to sacrifice our relationship as a test of our obedience to him. When he realised the extent to which we were willing to obey him, he gave it us all back with a little bit more! God restored our relationship, healed the hurt and blessed us six months later with engagement leading into marriage. I also got offered the job in 'tbc' and God has continued to bless us individually and as a couple since.

I'm not saying that God asks everyone to sacrifice something so precious. He wanted to teach Tim and me something, and he wanted to test us.

Prayer

Lord,

Thank you that we can trust you with our whole lives and you will never let us down. Thank you that no matter what does let us down, you will always be there to lift us up.

Forgive me, Jesus, for the times when I have tried to do things my own way instead of following your way. I'm sorry for not trusting you when I should have. Help me to trust you in everything I do.

In Jesus' name,

Amen.

How far are you prepared to go?

Let's take a look at Noah. He was another man with an astonishing job to do. The Lord had made the earth perfectly, but then humankind messed up. God was unhappy with what they were doing.

'So the LORD said, "I will destroy all human beings that I made on the earth. And I will destroy every animal and everything that crawls on the earth and the birds of the air, because I am sorry I have made them." But Noah pleased the LORD.'
(Genesis 6:7,8)

Why did Noah find favour with the Lord? What was it about Noah that made God choose him?

' ... Noah was a good man, the most innocent man of his time, and he walked with God.'
(Genesis 6:9)

Well, if that's not something for us to base our lives on then I'm not sure what is! That's why God used Noah: because his life reflected God in all areas. Not only did Noah have God's favour, but his attitude and lifestyle were pure and holy. He was also committed to doing God's will. Can you imagine someone coming up to you and asking you to build a 450-foot long boat and then putting two of every species on the boat and floating for 40 days? You'd think they were having a laugh! But Noah just did it.

God can use anyone at any time to do his will.

I think the encouraging bit is that Noah and Abraham were very old when God used them the most. That just shows that God can use anyone at any time to do his will. You're never too old or too young (see the story of Samuel's call for an example of a young person being used by God). The extent to which he uses you depends on you and how much you want to be used. If you don't allow God to take control, he won't. He isn't in the business of forcing his way into your life. It's got to be your choice.

The reality of a God-given promise

Moses was another man of God who was noted in history as a man of obedience. If you read about Moses, you'll notice that his life was full of ups and downs. He was a prince who became a pauper; he was a murderer who was forgiven in the eyes of God; he was a man who had a great calling on his life – to lead the Israelites out of Egypt and set the captives free.

I want to concentrate on one section of Moses' journey through the wilderness – the parting of the Red Sea.

' ... "You only need to remain calm; the LORD will fight for you."

Then the LORD said to Moses, "Why are you crying out to me? Command the Israelites to start moving. Raise your walking stick and hold it over the sea so that the sea will split and the people can cross it on dry land.'

(Exodus 14:14-16)

Imagine the pressure! Moses has been given the responsibility of parting the Red Sea and leading thousands of people through it. But Moses had so much faith in God that he did it. He knew that God had given him a specific calling. He trusted God, took a massive leap of faith and led his followers to freedom. Wow!

'When the Israelites saw the great power the LORD had used against the Egyptians, they feared the LORD, and they trusted him and his servant Moses.' (Exodus 14:31)

Why couldn't the Israelites just have trusted God in the first place – when he first gave them that promise of freedom? Why did they have to see him perform miracles first before they were convinced? God fulfilled his promise to Moses and the Israelites, just like he said he would.

I act in the same way as the Israelites sometimes. Even though I can see God working in my life and in other people's lives, I still find it hard to trust him. It's almost as if I'm saying to God, 'I'm not going to believe that until I see it happen.'

We don't like giving ourselves fully to anything because we are afraid of getting hurt.

Over the years, I have asked myself why we fail to trust others and I believe the answer is this: we don't give ourselves fully to anything because we are afraid of getting hurt. When I had my eating disorder, I put my trust in food because I thought it was never going to hurt me. Sometimes we don't like having to trust people because we are afraid of being let down. It's human instinct to protect ourselves. But that's when we need to get on to God's level. God will never let you down; he will never leave you to fight for yourself; he will never go back on his word; and he will never stop thinking about you and loving you. Just knowing that God is always there for us will help us to love and trust other people more openly – and maybe not to mind so much if they do let us down.

' ... the LORD's love surrounds those who trust him.'
(Psalm 32:10)

'We love because God first loved us.'
(1 John 4:19)

God's way not yours

I once had a massive turning-point about the trust and obedience issues of being a Christian teenager. It started with me moaning about not being able to get drunk and have sex and live a so-called normal life. I moaned about always being expected to be an example to other people and the pressure of having to live up to certain standards. I moaned about how hard it was to forgive people when you didn't want to forgive them, etc. I eventually came to the conclusion that being a Christian was too hard. But that's when I sensed God grabbing hold of me and saying, 'But, Shell, this is not about being a Christian. This is about having a relationship with me. This is about collecting all your fears, all your worries, all your anxieties, all your doubts and all your questions, dumping them at the foot of the cross, and moving on. This is not about you – this is about me! It's about how much you're prepared to give, in order to do my will. It's about how many times you're prepared to be stripped away in order to be renewed with my love and filled with my Holy Spirit. It is not always going to be easy and it is not always going to be comfortable, but I will bless you with the nations if you want them.'

Wow! You see, I didn't want to trust God. I wanted to know and I wanted to understand, but when we enter into a relationship with God we won't always be able to know and understand. However, we will always be able to trust God because he is always faithful to his promises.

'The Scriptures say that Abraham had two sons. The mother of one son was a slave woman, and the mother of the other son was a free woman. Abraham's son from the slave woman was born in the normal human way. But the son from the free woman was born because of the promise God made to Abraham.'

(Galatians 4:22,23)

Remember how Abraham so desperately wanted a son and God promised him that he would have a child of his own? Well, even Abraham, a great man of faith, found it difficult to trust God. He found it so difficult that he had sex with his slave. She got pregnant, gave birth to a baby boy and hey presto, Abraham had a son. He had sex with someone other than his wife so that he could have a son. He did it his own way.

Even though Abraham had done wrong, God didn't withhold his promise. He still gave Abraham and his wife Sarah, a son of their own, but in his timing.

'But what does the Scripture say? "Throw out the slave woman and her son. The son of the slave woman should not inherit anything. The son of the free woman should receive it all." So, my brothers and sisters, we are not children of the slave woman, but of the free woman.'

(Galatians 4:30,31)

Isaac, Abraham and Sarah were acceptable to God because of their faith. Even though Abraham did it his own way first, God restored his faith when Isaac was born. Therefore, Isaac will share the family inheritance (countless millions of people and nations). It just goes to show that when God makes a promise, there is nothing that can stand in the way of his fulfilling it. It may not make sense to us. We may not even understand what God is doing, but we can be sure that God will stay faithful in all circumstances.

When God makes a promise, there is nothing that can stand in the way of his fulfilling it!

'Trust the LORD with all your heart,
and don't depend on your own understanding.
Remember the LORD in all you do,
and he will give you success.'

(Proverbs 3:5,6)

Everything belongs to God

'The earth belongs to the LORD, and everything in it –
the world and all its people.
He built it on the waters
and set it on the rivers.
Who may go up on the mountain of the LORD?
Who may stand in his holy Temple?
Only those with clean hands and pure hearts,
who have not worshipped idols,
who have not made promises in the name of a false god.
They will receive a blessing from the LORD;
the God who saves them will declare them right.
They try to follow God;
they look to the God of Jacob for help.'

(Psalm 24:1-6)

Everything belongs to God. He can give and take away at any time. That's not to say that God is going to take away the things you love the most; it's just to make you realise that he could if he wanted to, because he's that big. Our attitude to possessions changes when we realise that all the things we have (possessions, home, family, friends, health, life itself) are actually gifts from God. Just knowing that makes me feel humbled and thankful for all that he has given me.

'Your heart will be where your treasure is.'

(Matthew 6:21)

'Don't store treasures for yourselves here on earth where moths and rust will destroy them and thieves can break in and steal them. But store your treasures in heaven where they cannot be destroyed by moths or rust and where thieves cannot break in and steal them. Your heart will be where your treasure is.'

(Matthew 6:19-21)

Prayer

Lord,

Thank you that you have given me the ability to be obedient to you. Thank you that you want what's best for me. Thank you that you're never going to leave me to fight things on my own.

Lord, I pray that I will have the faith of Abraham, the favour that Noah had and the courage and obedience of Moses. I want you to use me and I say to you this day, 'Here I am.'

I give everything I am and everything I have to you, and pray that you will use my life to glorify your holy name.

In the name of Jesus Christ, our Lord and Saviour, Amen.

A God of the impossible

I want to conclude this book with an amazing true-life story, to inspire you to have faith and trust in God and believe that he can work miracles in your own life.

My friend, Jess, suffered with ME for several years and spent all of her teenage life on crutches or in a wheelchair. ME is a syndrome that causes fatigue, muscle weakness and pains. Everyday life was difficult. She couldn't plan day-to-day activities and she was uncertain of her future, but the thing she held on to the most was her faith in God. She never blamed God for her illness, but she really wanted to be healed.

Things started to change for Jess when she stopped seeking healing and began to focus on God as a healer. She eventually felt that she wanted God even more than she wanted to be healed.

Jess heard about a women's day at Abundant Life Church in Bradford. It wasn't a day focused on healing, but she felt that somehow God was saying to her, 'This is your day.'

The whole day was based around the story of David and Goliath (see 1 Samuel 17 for the full story). Everyone was challenged to write down their 'Goliath' (in this instance, an obstacle they had to conquer) and throw it on to the altar. Jess wrote down her illness on the piece of paper and threw it on the altar.

As she sat there, she felt she heard God say really clearly, 'Put your crutches down and walk!' Then she began to shake and feel extremely close to God. She spent 20 minutes just sitting there, shaking and crying.

But she knew that this was her moment. This was the opportunity she had been waiting for and she didn't want it to pass her by. So she gathered herself together, put down her crutches, stood up and started to walk! Everyone was in shock at the power of God at work in her. He had undoubtedly healed her! She hadn't walked without crutches for several years and now God had enabled her to do the impossible!

The doctors couldn't explain what had happened.

Jess had to have a bit of physiotherapy for a while, to build up her muscles again. The doctors couldn't understand or explain what had happened. But Jess knew that God is an awesome God and a God of the impossible.

It was a strange few months for Jess. Suddenly, after being disabled for so long, she could walk. It was quite a challenge for her. She didn't have to be reliant on other people any more. It was an amazing feeling of freedom!

Being healed was like the beginning of a whole new life. Jess had an awesome experience of God that not everyone gets. But that doesn't mean to say that everything has been easy for her since. There are still tough times, but God did something in Jess' life that gives hope to others. No one can deny what God has done for her.

Prayer

Lord,

Thank you that you have the power and the ability to heal people from anything. Thank you that with your strength I have the ability to do anything.

I pray that you will increase the amount of faith I have. Help me to be more and more like you.

In the name of Jesus,

Amen.

Want to know more...?

A-Z of being a Girl of God *Dawn Reynolds-Deaville*

An inspirational and funky guide to living for God.

Scripture Union 1 85999 764 3

Conclusion

I hope that this book has challenged you and encouraged you in your relationship with God. Know that whatever situation you may find yourself in, good or bad, present or future, God loves you no matter what. He thinks you're amazing and nothing you do will ever change that.

Stay close to the one who loves you the most!

Love and laughs

References:

Mellin, L, McNutt, S, Hu, Y, Schreiber, G.B., Crawford, P.,& Obarzanek, E. (1991) A longitudinal study of the dietary practices of black and white girls 9-and 10-years-old at enrolment: The NHLBI growth and health study. Journal of Adolescent Health, 27-37.

Smolak, L., (1996). National Eating Disorders Association/ Next Door Neighbours puppet guide book.

"Who Do You Think You Are?" by Steve Mawston. (Scripture Union 1997)

"If You Want to Walk on Water You've Got to Get Out of the Boat" by John Ortberg. 2001 Zondervan Michigan

AIDS: The Dawn of Fear US News and World Report, 12 January 1987

What part will you play in God's mission to a world in need?

You are a vital piece in God's mission jigsaw, just waiting to be placed in a you-shaped gap.

Get involved!

There's plenty of action right here with Scripture Union. And it involves children and young people. Thousands will visit a Scripture Union mission or go on a Scripture Union holiday this year. Many will experience God's love for the first time. Others will make great leaps in their faith.

How? Through people like you who give some of their time to join a Scripture Union team. Mission and holiday teams play a key role, sharing God's love with children and young people.

It's about building relationships. It's about being a team. It's about being available to allow God's Spirit to work to change lives.

For some of us, this may mean giving a week or so during our holidays. Others may have a gap year ahead, in which case you could consider one of our international placements serving God overseas. (Please note that you need to be at least 16 to serve on a holiday or mission team, and between 18 and 25 to go on an international placement.)

For more information about these exciting opportunities, please go to www.scriptureunion.org.uk, email info@scriptureunion.org.uk or telephone 01908 856000 during office hours.

A note from Innervation Trust

Innervation's ultimate intention is to make the gospel explode onto the scene in a language that young people can understand and relate to. The dream… for every secondary school in the UK to have access to a quality schools' band!

'thebandwithnoname' and 'tbc' are the Innervation touring bands. They are responsible for blitzing the world with the Gospel of Jesus Christ, raising the awareness of Innervation, fundraising for Innervation, and recruiting young talented people for the schools' bands. These bands are then dedicated to their specific counties, doing exciting schools' weeks including: RE lessons, lunchtime concerts, and Friday night events where the young people have an opportunity to respond to the Gospel.

The best thing about Innervation is that it's already working! Thousands upon thousands of young people are hearing about God and responding to his message.

How you can get involved…

You too can be part of this amazing vision! We are looking for young, talented evangelists aged 17+ to join Innervation and be part of the network of schools' bands. If you think you've got what it takes, please email Innervation: info@innervation.org

Innervation depends on both your prayer and financial support in order to continue its work. If you would like to become an Innervation supporter, please contact us via our website: www.innervation.org or email us directly at info@innervation.org

Hear Shell on TBC's fantastic CD

Cat number: 1908352

You and God

Elaine Carr

You want to talk to God, right? And being able to listen to him would be pretty cool too. But does doing it regularly seem impossible?! Do you just pray the same things every single time?

This book is guaranteed (well, almost!) to help you talk with God every day. It also gives you great advice on what to do if your mind's wandering, if you can't keep going, and how to pray in difficult situations. There's bags of space for you to write in your own experiences and ideas and there's even a great way to keep track of your prayers so you can see how God's answering them!

ISBN: 1 84427 025 4

Under Pressure

Claire Pedrick + Andy Morgan

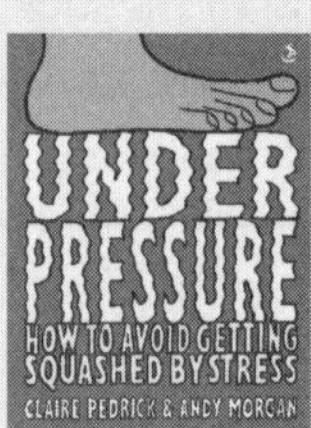

exams? parents? doubt? body stuff? money? green issues? drugs? other religions? rivalry? prayer? STRESS?!

There's so much going on that gives us stress, but this book will help you sort through some ways of dealing with it. Whether it's worrying about exams or getting het up about spots this fantastic new handbook helps you deal with the stuff that really puts you under pressure.

ISBN: 1 84427 008 4